The beginner's guide to
FLORISTRY

The beginner's guide to
FLORISTRY

REVISED EDITION

ROSEMARY BATHO
JUDI KAY
BERNICE WAUGH

YORK

MURDOCH
B O O K S

The combinations of flowers and foliage featured in this
book are intended to whet the creative appetite and
on to further ideas – please enjoy experimenting
and substituting alternative materials, according to what
is available at the time and suitable for the
particular end use of any design or arrangement.

First published in 1998 by Murdoch Books UK Ltd
Merehurst is an imprint of Murdoch Books UK Ltd
Ferry House, 51-57 Lacy Road, Putney, London SW15 1PR
Copyright © 1994 Merehurst Limited
Reprinted 1995, 1996, 1997, 2003, 2004 (twice)
Revised Edition 1998

ISBN 1-85391-787-7

A catalogue record of this book is available from the British Library.

The publisher has made every effort to ensure that all instructions
given in this book are safe and accurate, but they cannot accept
liability for any resulting injury, loss or damage to either property
or person whether direct or consequential and howsoever arising.
The authors and publishers will be grateful for any information
which will assist them in keeping future editions up to date.

Commissioning Editors: Heather Dewhurst and Karen Hemingway
Editor: Diana Lodge
Designers: Cooper Wilson Design and Anita Ruddell
Photographer: Karl Adamson

Chief Executive: Juliet Rogers
Publisher: Kay Scarlett

Colour Separation by Bright Arts (HK) Ltd
Printed in Singapore by CS Graphics

Front cover: Bridal bouquet featuring *Phalaenopsis* orchids,
Exochorda x *macrantha* 'The Bride', *Leucojum*, *Mahonia* x *media* berries,
Stephanotis floribunda, *Tulipa* 'Buttermilk', *Rosa* 'Princess',
Trachelium caeruleum, *Asparagus setaceus*, *Helleborus orientalis*,
Convallaria majalis and brassica flowers.

CONTENTS

LESSON 6, *Page 116*

DRIED AND FABRIC FLOWERS

LESSON 7, *Page 140*

WEDDING FLOWERS

INTRODUCTION

Floristry is a fascinating, varied and creative profession, which combines a wide range of skills, techniques and specialist knowledge. *The Beginner's Guide to Floristry* contains the fundamental information required to assist student florists of all ages in their training.

Being able carefully and sensitively to advise customers in times of sadness and happiness is one of the florist's greatest skills. Flowers and foliage, artistically arranged, can be used for many different occasions – to celebrate a birth, mark an anniversary, offer congratulations on passing an exam, or wish someone a happy birthday. Beautiful funeral tributes bring comfort and express respect. Today's bride can choose from a wide range of designs and styles offered by her florist.

The florist's calendar is filled with special occasions, including the traditional favourites of Christmas, Valentine's Day and Mother's Day. Other annual celebrations, including New Year, Easter, Hallowe'en and the saints' days, can all be celebrated with flowers.

Today, the creative possibilities are endless, and the professional florist needs to master the basic techniques and skills, for without this sound knowledge it would be impractical to progress to advanced and free-style designs.

Colourful, unusual, delicate and exotic are just some of the words used to describe the fantastic range of flowers and foliage types now available. Appropriate handling of these materials takes skill and knowledge. A florist with the ability to give the general public aftercare advice and special tips will attract customers who appreciate expertise.

Now, more than ever before, it is necessary to be aware of and ready to accept new technology, which is changing the working practises in the florist's shop. Traditional wiring methods and construction techniques are being superseded by glue products and their various applicators. Nevertheless, it is essential for the trained florist to be able to use traditional methods, as they still have their uses on occasion and form part of the basic repertoire of skills.

For those who wish to pursue a career in the floristry industry, the confidence gained from a sound foundation cannot be overstated. From basic training come the standards and techniques that will last a lifetime.

The beauty of flowers enhances many occasions – here Casablanca Lilies in a bouquet capture a happy wedding day.

CARE OF CUT FLOWERS

In the last ten years there has been a considerable increase in consumer purchases of cut flowers. Worldwide, sales of stems can be numbered in billions. Mirroring this growth in the flower industry has been extensive scientific research into the post-harvest care of cut flowers and foliage.

This chapter presents a concise florists' guide to flower-handling. It deals with the availability of cut flowers; the correct stage at which to buy; correct storage procedures and, finally, offering aftercare advice to the customer. For many customers, the quality of flowers is determined by their longevity; the professional florist will ensure that cut flowers achieve their maximum vase life.

THE WORLD MARKET

Kenya, the French Riviera, Israel – the cut flowers and foliage sold in shops and stores come from almost every part of the world. Tulips from England and the Netherlands sit in vases next to carnations flown in from Colombia, Turkey or Italy.

The availability of cut flowers and foliage has expanded dramatically over the last twenty years, and the number of countries that grow and export cut materials continues to increase. Several factors have contributed to this growth: faster and better methods of transport, including air freight, ensure that flowers are kept at optimum temperatures during their journey; sophisticated packaging methods enable even delicate flowers to reach their destination in perfect condition, and the use of pre-treatments and flower foods has increased the life of cut materials.

Countries producing cut flowers fall into several categories: those with a high consumer demand, such as the USA or Japan; areas with favourable climates, such as Israel, the Canary Islands or Spain, and countries such as Kenya, Turkey or Mexico, where the overheads are low. This list increases alongside technological advances.

National markets

The world's major producers and buyers of cut flowers are the Japanese. In Britain, in contrast, fewer flowers are bought than in other European countries. In spite of this, British florists buy their flowers from a wide range of international suppliers, as do florists the world over.

Covent Garden, adjacent to the Royal Opera House in London, was Britain's most

Our plants and flowers come from all over the world.
Right *Plants for seasonal tubs and baskets.* **Below** *New Covent Garden market.*
Centre *Chrysanthemums grown for nearby florists and larger markets.* **Far right, above and below** *The Flying Dutchman (courtesy of the Flower Council of Holland).*

famous fruit, flower and vegetable market until 1974. In that year, the New Covent Garden Market was opened, superseding the old one, and it is from here that many florists buy flowers and foliage, imported from around the world. Other flower markets are situated up and down the country, and by the time that the general public are starting to get up, florists are already on their way back to their businesses, having selected and purchased the best buys of the day. Florists in rural areas rely on local growers or van salesmen. The Flying Dutchman, bringing flowers from the Dutch auctions, is a familiar sight in Britain.

Flowers from local growers can have the advantages of less packaging, for a shorter journey, and a 'just cut' freshness, as florists can literally pick flowers from local growers.

Each country has its own national suppliers. In Britain, for example, several regions are well known for their flower production, including Lincolnshire, Cornwall and the Channel Islands, and when daffodils arrive in boxes from cool Scotland, the British florist knows that the daffodil season is almost at an end.

The Dutch auctions
Flowers sold in Dutch auctions come from many countries, so the Dutch offer the most comprehensive range of cut materials to be found anywhere in the world.

The ten flower auctions in Holland use a 'clock' system, whereby prices fluctuate daily, according to demand. The high demand before Mother's Day, for example, results in correspondingly high prices.

HARVESTING AND PACKAGING

The care of cut flowers begins long before the florist has come on the scene, even before the grower has planted the seed or cuttings – it starts in the laboratory. It is here that flowers and foliages are examined and analysed in minute detail, and it is here that many old wives' tales have been either disproved or, perhaps more interestingly, supported and improved upon.

As a result of extensive scientific research, primarily in the Netherlands, growers know with precision the most favourable time to harvest a flower crop so that it will give maximum value to the customer. Cut too soon, and the buds will not open and develop; cut too late, and the flowers will be past their best too quickly. Once harvested, many varieties of cut flower are then pre-treated to ensure maximum vase life.

Pre-treatments, discussed in further detail on pages 32-3, are products added to the water so that they enter the flower stems, preventing the effects of ethylene and prolonging vase life. It is compulsory for many cut flowers that pass through Dutch auctions to be pre-treated, thus ensuring them a longer life for the consumer to enjoy.

Ethylene
This is an odourless gas that is also a natural plant hormone. It is generated by all plant parts, some of the gas being released into the surrounding air, in particular, when a plant is stressed or physically damaged. The more ethylene in the air, the earlier the cut flowers will mature, giving less pleasure and value to the customer. It can be found in less attractive environments – in car exhaust fumes and cigarette smoke, for example – and is also given off by rubbish, fungi, bacteria and ripening fruit.

So what is the effect of this natural plant hormone? Some flowers are more susceptible than others, carnations showing perhaps the most dramatic effects. Stored at room temperature with ripe tomatoes or apples, untreated carnations can wither overnight. Other symptoms are yellowing leaves and leaf drop, and the failure of buds to develop. Ethylene-sensitive flowers include alstroemeria, roses, most species of *Dianthus*, freesias and several others.

Flowers that have been given a pre-treatment are less sensitive to ethylene; more buds open, and their vase life is extended by between 50 and 75 per cent, when compared with the vase life of untreated flowers.

Bacteria
Bacteria are also of concern to florists, because they can block the water-carrying vessels and prevent the uptake of water and nutrients. This results in flowers wilting prematurely, and failing to achieve their full potential. Prevention is dealt with later in the chapter.

Arrival at the florist's shop
Thanks to the packaging methods now used by growers and exporters, flowers should arrive in the best possible condition. Many flowers are now aqua packed or wet packed for transport. This is an excellent method, as the stem ends do not dry out and instead have a constant supply of water and flower preservative.

Most spray carnations are now sold in buckets enclosed by a box to keep them upright. For many years, orchids have had test tubes with a small reservoir of water attached to stem ends, and freesias are often supplied with a wad of damp absorbent paper attached.

Foliage from distant countries, such as Costa Rica, arrives in perfect condition, enclosed as it now is in sheets of polythene within strong boxes. The polythene keeps the foliage in the conditions of high humidity that most foliage types prefer. Mimosa also requires high humidity around its fluffy flowers, and is sold in individually sealed bags.

Alstroemeria, chrysanthemums and other flowers are enclosed in cellophane sleeves and packed in boxes to prevent movement during transit. The cellophane also slows down transpiration and evaporation of water from the foliage and flowers, creating a moist and humid atmosphere. Gerberas, with their delicate petals, have an inner sleeve in the box so that each flower head is held quite still. Anthuriums (flamingo flowers) are held in their box and packed with soft paper straw to cushion the beautiful bracts.

Good packaging protects flowers during transit from distant countries, ensuring they arrive at the florist's shop in good condition, with the minimum of damage.

CONDITIONING TECHNIQUES

If cut flowers are to give good value for money – to you and to your customers – it is important to ensure that they are properly cared for. As with other kinds of stock, routine preparations should be made before the arrival of each consignment of cut flowers.

Advance preparations

Make sure there is a clear area where the flower boxes and bunches can be stacked, with enough room to allow the stock to be conditioned. Check that you will be able to dispose of rubbish and packaging efficiently. Prepare clean stock buckets in a range of sizes, filling them with tepid water and the correct amount of cut flower food.

All the necessary tools and equipment – knife, secateurs, scissors, gloves, cloths, dustpan and brush – should be readily to hand. It is important that all equipment is clean. Use a proprietary cleaner or weak household bleach to clean buckets, worktops, knives and scissors.

Initial checks

As the flowers arrive, make a quick visual inspection to ensure that the stock tallies with the order. Stack the boxes neatly, with the delicate materials on top. Any loose flower packs should be put on the worktop, never on the floor.

Unpack and condition systematically, using the appropriate method for each cut material (see pages 19-23). All flowers should be healthy and in good condition, so check for pests, broken stems or flower heads, and temperature damage. Report any problems to the wholesaler.

Once flowers and foliage are in water, they can be stored in a cool room or fridge (see page 30). If possible, flowers should have from four to six hours to recover from the stresses of transit before being sold. Wipe the worktop, sweep the floor, and remove any rubbish from around the conditioning flowers.

Stem blockages

Before detailing the conditioning methods, it is appropriate to know how stems can get blocked, which prevents them taking up water and food. Cut flowers lose water through the stomata in the foliage (these can be likened to skin pores) and through petals. This is part of the process called transpiration, and the lost water must be replaced through the stems – and in a few cases, leaves – or wilting will occur.

Water and food is taken up the stem to the leaves and petals by water-conducting vessels. When a stem is cut, transpiration continues, but the stem takes up air, which forms a pocket or embolism that impedes and can entirely obstruct the transport of water. The florist deals with these air pockets by cutting away a short length from the bottom of each stem and placing stems in water immediately afterwards. Rapid water loss is further checked by keeping the flowers in a cool place, with high relative humidity.

Preventing bacterial growth

Stems can additionally be blocked by bacteria. The growth of these micro-organisms in the water and inside the stems can cause serious problems to sensitive flowers such as gerberas and roses.

A clean wound surface is essential, as damaged cells rot faster, and the end result is decay and the spread of bacteria that will pollute the water.

Unpleasant smells can develop as the cells in foliage below the waterline collapse. As the bacteria continue to grow, the stem ends – damaged stem ends in particular – become slimy and disagreeable to handle. This, in turn, leads to premature wilting of flowers and foliage.

To avoid this offensive scenario, florists use flower preservatives (page 32) which contain a disinfectant that will inhibit the growth of bacteria.

It is also important to remove foliage that will lie below the waterline. A clean, sharp knife is another essential (a knife will not damage the stem cells as much as scissors, which pinch or bruise the stem). Clean buckets and clean water help to ensure that cut flowers get a bacteria-free start on arrival at their destination. Cold storage and low temperatures will inhibit the growth and development of bacteria.

Customers purchasing flowers can help prevent premature wilting by putting flowers into water as quickly as possible, and not leaving them too long in a car, especially in warm weather.

Conditioning

Conditioning is the treatment given to cut flowers and foliage in order to encourage the uptake of water and ensure that the vase life is as long as possible.

The general procedure is as follows: remove the packaging and then cut away any foliage that will fall below the waterline; groom the materials, removing damaged foliage, petals or flower heads; cut 2.5-5cm (1-2in) from the stem, cutting diagonally and using a sharp knife (not scissors), and place the materials immediately into prepared tepid water.

An angled cut prevents the stem end from standing flat on the container bottom, impeding the water supply.

Stem structures

Cut materials display a variety of stem types. Florists divide these into different categories – soft stems, firm stems, woody stems, hollow stems and latex-producing stems (see page 21).

Various methods can be used to encourage the uptake of water, the choice depending on the type of stem. The warm water method is particularly useful for soft and firm stems, for dry-packed materials, for tropical flowers, and for flowers in tight bud. The procedure is the same as that already mentioned, except that the container is filled with warm (35-40°C/95-104°F) water, rather than tepid, along with the correct amount of plant food.

In the picture is a selection of materials that are easy to cut and are generally called soft stemmed – chincherinchee, daffodil, nerine, alstroemeria, gerbera, anemone and tulip. Individual flower requirements are discussed later in this section.

These firm-stemmed materials benefit from the warm water method of treatment. Warm water contains fewer air bubbles and is taken up the stem faster. Pictured are spray orchids, carnations, chrysanthemums, bear grass and leatherleaf.

SPECIALIST METHODS

Flowers arrive in the flower shop in bunches, boxes, buckets and wraps of cellophane, and tied up in bundles. What is conditioned first?

Conditioning priorities

Wilted flowers should always be conditioned first. They will need the longest time to recover, and if you leave their conditioning until last they may become unsaleable.

The last flowers to require conditioning are those that have arrived 'aqua packed'; several types of cut material are now being transported in this way to reduce the problems inevitably involved in transporting living, and short-lived, flowers.

Between these categories, there are others that will also require priority treatment. The delicate and generally expensive flowers such as orchids, lilies and roses should be conditioned and stored quickly, to prevent the accidental damage that might occur if they were left until last. Cut materials that are required for customers' orders should also be treated promptly, to allow them suf-

ficient time for a good drink of water and flower food before use. The other category of cut material requiring speedy treatment consists of those that have been 'dry packed'. These will need several hours to recover before being displayed for sale. Aqua-packed materials, on the other hand, can be ready for sale in just two to four hours.

Once the priorities have been established, the flowers and foliage can be treated according to the stem structure; whether the materials are flaccid and wilted, or perhaps the particular requirements of the individual cut flower or foliage (for further details, see page 250). The following methods are very useful in encouraging 'difficult' materials to take up water. (The warm water method has been explained on page 19.)

Boiling water

Remove the lower foliage; protect the flower heads with cellophane or paper and cut the stem ends, making a slanted cut and using a sharp knife.

Immediately plunge the stem ends into boiling water, 2.5cm (1in) deep. Keep them there for one minute, and then top up the water with tepid water to which a flower food has been added. The boiling water should remove any air in the stem, making it easier for water to be taken up. This technique also has the advantage that only a minimal amount of bacteria will be left alive to grow on the stem ends.

This is a useful method for hard, woody stems, such as lilac, prunus, and other tree and shrub materials. It can also be used for wilted flowers – roses, for example – and for those stems of the Euphorbia family that contain a milky sap called latex.

Searing or singeing

This treatment is reserved exclusively for those stems that exude a milky sap – poppies, for example, or euphorbias. It is not the most straightforward of methods, and is not often used, the boiling-water method being the simpler one and therefore generally preferred.

Woody-stemmed materials, of which a selection is shown here, can prove difficult to condition. Use warm water and flower food or, if necessary, the boiling-water method, to encourage uptake.

Remove the lower foliage (wear gloves, as the sap can be an irritant when in contact with skin); protect the flower heads, as for the boiling-water method, and pass the stem ends through a flame – gas, candle or match. Place immediately into tepid water to which flower food has been added.

The charcoal layer that forms on the bottom of the stem allows water through, but prevents the milky sap from leaking out and polluting the water.

Hollow stems

Flowers with hollow stems, such as delphinium hybrids, can be inverted and filled with water from a watering can. Plug the end with cotton wool and place the stem in a bucket of tepid water. The cotton wool acts as a wick, and the water in the stem will keep the whole flower turgid.

Stock rotation

Good stock rotation is essential in a flower shop, ensuring that waste is kept to a minimum. In addition to minimizing waste, and therefore helping to increase profits, an efficient stock rotation will help to ensure that the flowers sold are always fresh. A good cool room routine is an important factor here. Keep new and old flowers separate, using the older stock first; check the cut materials each day; some flowers, such as stock and larkspur, will require a daily change of water, while others may need to be tidied, and some stem ends will need recutting. Provide plenty of space; this will reduce breakages and prevent the build-up of botrytis and moulds.

To ensure good straight stems, support gerberas while they are being conditioned. A simple method is to use the packaging material.

Passing the stem ends of flowers such as Euphorbia fulgens *through a candle flame prevents the milky sap from leaking out.*

FURTHER TECHNIQUES

Immersion

Some cut materials can absorb water through the epidermal cells surrounding the stem and leaves. This method of complementing water taken up by the roots has led to the development of foliar feeds.

Violets have the additional advantage of a cuticle that is less restricting than that of other plants. The cuticle is a waxy, water-proof layer, exuded by the epidermis. Holly and laurel have tough cuticles, whereas violets, rose leaves and new foliage have thin cuticles. Florists take advantage of these facts when preparing cut materials.

Immersion in tepid water is beneficial for violets, some tropical flowers, soft, young foliage, and wilted materials. Petals can be damaged by prolonged immersion, so this should only be for a short time – some ten to twenty minutes would be sufficient for anthuriums and dendrobiums, or an hour for violets, young foliages and wilted flowers, such as roses.

Hairy leaves should not be submerged, and nor should grey foliage, which will loose its colour until it has dried out. Waxy and fleshy flowers should not be submerged, as they will discolour and stain.

Humidity

An increase in the relative humidity around cut materials is beneficial to most flowers, and to some it is very important. If the water loss through petals and foliage exceeds the rate at which water is taken up through the stem, then the cut material will wilt. Many cut materials are wrapped in cellophane sleeves in order to reduce this transpiration. Regularly spraying materials with water will also help to reduce the water loss, particularly if the atmosphere is warm and dry, or if there is a constant draught of air, from a doorway, perhaps, or from air conditioning.

Mimosa and tropical flowers will benefit from regular misting, as will cut foliages, such as *Codiaem* (Joseph's coat), *Nephrolepis* (sword fern), and – though its name may suggest otherwise – leatherleaf, which is a type of shield fern.

High humidity is also advantageous to flowers that have a much greater petal surface than stem surface, such as hydrangeas, roses, and many other summer flowers. Transpiration can be further diminished by removing some of the foliage, ensuring that water will reach the flower head rather than superfluous leaves.

1 *These roses are showing signs of water distress. The necks are bent and the foliage is flaccid. Re-cut the stems and immerse in tepid water.*

2 *After one hour, the roses are wrapped in paper to keep the stems straight and are placed in a container of deep water with added flower food.*

3 *Completely revived, these 'Sonia' roses can be arranged. Keep them out of direct sunlight, and mist them regularly with water.*

Speeding up development

Spring-flowering shrubs have already formed their flower buds as they enter dormancy. Trees and shrubs such as hazel (catkins), forsythia, lilac, cherry, almond, and cytisus (broom) can be encouraged to flower much earlier. A florist who has a ready supply of such materials can make good use of this technique.

The shrub material requires a lengthy period of cold before the buds will open, so it is not practical to cut before January. (In Germany, where the cold weather can start in December, it was an old tradition to use blossoming branches as a Christmas decoration.) The stems are placed into buckets of warm water with a cut flower food. It can take three weeks before the buds start to open, but the later in the season the shrubs are cut, the faster the buds will open.

If they are needed fully open, tight flower buds can be encouraged by the same method. Warm water, prepared with flower food, good light, and a warm room temperature will speed development to the required stage.

Slowing down

There are times during the seasons when it may be advantageous to 'hold' the development of a flower, perhaps to even out a glut of flowers, or before a peak sales period. Tulips, gladioli and peonies are especially suited to the following method.

It is essential to use flowers that are in good condition, showing no signs of mould or fungal diseases, so a thorough inspection is recommended. If the cut flowers are flaccid, they will need a drink to regain firmness before storage. Excess foliage is removed and bunches can be re-wrapped in paper. Shake off surplus water. Cellophane should not be used, as it can induce moulds. Once wrapped, the bunches are carefully packed into boxes.

Placed in the cold store, or in a cold dark cellar, the flowers can be kept for five to seven days, and conditioned in the normal way when required.

Freshly-cut Cytisus x praecox *(broom), as compared with the species cut and forced for ten days in February. The later in the season the sprays are cut, the faster the flower buds will open.*

Golden 'Apeldoorn' tulips in cellophane, ready for inspection, and wrapped in paper for eventual cold storage. Cold storage will slow down the processes in the cut materials.

SPRING FLOWERS

Spring starts early in a florist's shop – the first daffodils can be found in the cool months of autumn, and tulips follow on just a few weeks later. Even so, it is still in the true springtime months that the bulk of spring flowers are sold.

With so many flowers now available out of season, it is scarcely surprising that many young florists become confused about the 'natural' seasons. Observing the flowering times in local gardens is a practical way of overcoming this difficulty.

In addition to the early flowers, florists have a core of flowers that are available in the shop every day of the year, among which roses and spray chrysanthemums are prime examples, but it is a joy to see and smell the first flowers of the season. The early daffodils, with their small flower heads

and abundance of natural foliage, are always a particular pleasure. Mimosa, with its spicy scent, hyacinths, double tulips, muscari and, later on in the season, lilac, violets, and the creamy-green guelder rose, all lend to spring arrangements the infinite variety that makes floristry so interesting.

Caring for spring flowers

When caring for spring flowers, it is useful to remember their natural flowering times. Spring can be a cold time of the year, and most spring flowers – especially the bulb flowers – will last longer if they are kept in the cool conditions of their natural habitat. Be aware, however, of those bulb flowers that need warmer conditions, such as amaryllis, which should not be refrigerated. Spring flowers need plenty of water, so

buckets and vases will all need a regular topping up. Other problems can occur if wrappings are left on for too long, or are too tight.

Tulips, freesias and mimosa are particularly susceptible. Moisture on foliage and petals can lead to spotting, and moulds may thrive.

By the middle of the season, flowering shrub materials are freely available. Lilac, forsythia, almond and pussy willow are all part of the wide range of spring flowers. A sharp knife is needed to cut the very hard stems, and hot-water treatment may be used to encourage the water uptake.

Arum lilies – 'the flowers of the field' – are very popular in church decorations, and their high price makes it well worth taking special care of them. The stem ends are very fleshy and can curl on the bottom of the

bucket, shortening the length of the stem; an elastic band around the stem ends will prevent this. The spathes are very delicate, and care must be taken not to bruise or knock them as they unfurl.

Special bulb and shrub flower foods ensure that spring flowers will give your customers the joys of spring.

Immature flowers

Early in the season, it is important to inspect cut materials carefully, and to gauge their maturity – flowers that are too immature will not develop properly. Daffodils and irises sold early in the season should be showing colour; later, nearer their natural flowering time, they can be in tight bud. Another guide to the quality of daffodils is weight, so heavier boxes command a premium price at auctions and markets.

SUMMER FLOWERS

Stocks, sunflowers, snapdragons and larkspur – some of the loveliest of the summer flowers are now available for much longer than just the summer months.

There is a profusion of flowers available throughout the summer season; varieties have been improved, and many are pre-treated to prevent petal drop in the summer heat. Larkspur was once notorious for leaving florists with very pretty confetti and bare stalks. Thanks to research, we can now be sure our summer flowers have a good vase life.

Like all other flowers, summer flowers cannot tolerate direct sunlight, and during the summer, the sun's rays can be harsh, particularly behind the shop window. Shop interiors should be cool, with dispersed light, and canopies are useful in keeping the sun at bay. Vases need daily checking, and thirsty cut materials will need regular topping up. Flowers such as eustoma and dahlias have stems that decay quickly in water, and they will need to be recut and have their water changed regularly, to prevent smells.

The colours available in summer flowers are as profuse as the varieties. Sweet peas come in a range of blues, whites, purples, red and pinks, from the softest shell pink to deepest crimson. The fiery oranges and rich yellows of the marigolds contrast with the soft cool green of lady's mantle, and on the hottest of summer days there are plenty of flowers to choose for a refreshing design in blues and white.

The shapes and textures of cut materials are also diverse, including tiny lavender spikes, the large spears of the red hot poker, rounded hydrangea heads, and lilies, with their pointed petals. At this time of year, there is a selection for every type of design, and numerous possible containers from which to choose, always bearing in mind that the latter need to be sufficiently large to hold a good-sized reservoir of water for thirsty summer flowers.

Pictured is a small selection from the very wide range of summer flowers, many of them once found in country cottage gardens, which are now available to florists.

AUTUMN AND WINTER FLOWERS

Nostalgia seems to pervade the florist's shop during the autumn months. Although they are available all the year round, rust and bronze chrysanthemum blooms and sprays epitomize autumn, but many seasonal flowers are associated with this time of year, including dahlias, with their rich colours and varied shapes, golden rod, and the slightly more exotic criniums, with their delicate pink trumpets.

Cereals, such as wheat and barley, are appropriate for harvest festival designs, and although traditional arrangements remain popular, modern arrangements lend themselves particularly well to the varied textures of vegetables, berries and fruits, and many new churches require the bold lines of a modern design to complement the décor.

Winter

Flowers associated with winter include hellebores which, although not generally available as a cut flower, can be purchased as pot plants. This is also true of the poinsettia, which will last much longer if the roots can be retained. Poinsettias are now available in pinks and creamy whites as well as scarlet, and combine beautifully with red carnations and carnation sprays.
The early spring flowers

can be teamed with some of the flowering winter branches, such as witch hazel or *Viburnum* x *bodnantense*.

Conditioning

When buying outdoor seasonal materials, watch for signs of damage from diseases or pests. Insects will also find homes in the centres of dahlias. Avoid cold winds when transporting autumn and winter flowers from the market to the shop. Designs can suffer from cold burn just going from shop to van, so it is essential to wrap and pack with care.

Display flowers outside the shop only on mild days, selecting those that have protective wraps whenever possible. Daffodils can generally withstand relatively low temperatures, but even they will suffer in bitingly cold winds.

The first narcissi and tulips appear in winter, and these and other spring flowers help to brighten the dark winter days. The spicy scent of hyacinths makes them a favourite, and the delicate beauty of snowdrops is a very special pleasure.

EXOTIC FLOWERS

Strange and unusual shapes, strong vibrant colours and interesting names characterize exotic flowers. Many of these are now imported from such diverse countries as New Guinea, the West Indies, Singapore, South Africa and Hawaii.

In general, exotic flowers have a long vase life, a crucial factor when you consider the huge distances that some of them must cover in order to reach their destinations. The use of air freight, efficient packaging and increasingly skilful and scientific post-harvest techniques means that these flowers and other plant materials are transported much faster than they used to be, and will therefore last even longer.

Species

Some of the flowers described as exotic are now regularly to be seen in florists' shops. Dendrobium orchids, kangaroo paws, wax flowers and gerberas are now popular with customers and can be used in a wide range of designs to stunning effect.

Other species are not seen quite so often, including the bird of paradise – a lovely name for *Strelitzia reginae*. Heliconias, with their rather odd names, such as 'Lobster Claw', 'Manoa Midnight' and 'Yellow Christmas', flower in colours ranging from lavender, orange, green and yellow through to dark red and almost black. One of the most recent arrivals, from South-East Asia, is the curcuma, a lilac-purple plant, with colourful bracts that resemble the ginger flower, and which, along with proteas and anthuriums, displays the excellent lasting qualities of tropical flowers.

Several of the flowers and foliage types shown here are cold-sensitive, and should not be put into cold store, but kept at room temperature. Orchids and other exotic materials are valued for their long life, bold forms, strong colours and interesting textures.

STORAGE

Refrigeration

A good florist will help flowers to achieve their maximum vase life. Sensible use of a chiller unit at night, at weekends, and during conditioning will help to slow the development of many cut materials.

Traditionally, florists' shops were situated on the shady side of the street, and they always had cool interiors, perhaps with a cold, dark cellar in which to store flowers. The reasons were not always fully understood, and it is worth explaining them in detail.

The production of ethylene, the ageing hormone, is slowed at low temperatures. Good air circulation, to prevent concentrations of gas, combined with pre-treatments and flower foods, lessens the problems of ethylene considerably. Ethylene filters, a new product, can be fitted in a chiller to 'clean' the air.

The low temperature and high humidity – 85-95 per cent is recommended – will help to reduce transpiration. A humidity gauge or hydrometer in the flower cooler will enable regular measurements to be taken. Air circulation is important, as mentioned above, but a slow speed of chilled air is desirable if water loss is to be kept low. The stomata, from which the water is lost, close in darkness, which further reduces the rate of transpiration.

The growth of bacteria is also slowed by low temperatures. Bacteria can contaminate the water and impede the water supply to the flower head.

Temperatures

The temperature requirements of species differ, and while many spring flowers will keep best at 2°C (35°F), others, such as carnations, prefer a minimum low of 8°C (46°F). Most florists find that an average chiller temperature of 6-8°C (42-46°F) is acceptable. It must also be remembered that many tropical flowers do not require cool storage, although they do enjoy high humidity – gingers, strelitzias, anthuriums and many orchids fall into this category. Cold-sensitive flowers can exhibit symptoms of 'bluestain' on the petals. Nerines, in particular, are susceptible to temperatures below 2°C (35°F). Euphorbia, heliconias and eucharis lilies are all materials that prefer a warmer storage temperature, and for these, and other tropical flowers and foliages, the temperature should preferably not fall below 16°C (60°F). High temperatures, however, will hasten the development of cut materials and shorten their vase life.

An even temperature should always be maintained, whether flowers are stored in a chiller unit or in a cool place. Wild fluctuations in temperature can cause discoloration in some flowers. Red roses are particularly sensitive to major temperature changes, and this is evident when petals take on a blue tinge.

Stock rotation

An efficient stock rotation system is essential if you are to ensure that fresh flowers are always sold and any waste is kept to an inevitable minimum.

Mature stock is used in designs such as sympathy designs, wedding flowers and window displays, which require the impact of developed flowers. Contracts, gift arrangements and the public require flowers that will develop and mature over a longer period.

To maintain the cut materials in the best condition, a cool room routine needs to be established. Flowers and foliage should be inspected each day. Thirsty flowers may need topping up, and blooms such as larkspur and stock need their water changed on a daily basis. Stems may need recutting, and broken stems, heads and foliage will need to be removed. As flowers open, they may require more space, to reduce breakages and to ensure a good circulation of fresh air. Buckets and containers of flowers should not stand too closely together for these reasons.

It is generally advisable not to mix different cut materials in one container; recently-cut daffodils, in particular, exude a slime that can be harmful to other flowers. The use of a special cut flower food will overcome this problem for customers.

It can be seen that flower care is not something that can be mastered overnight. Experience with flowers and foliage types is fundamental to successful floristry, as is a knowledge of the processes that take place once a flower is cut.

Chiller units help to slow down the process that can speed development of flowers and foliage.

FOODS AND AFTERCARE

Food, provided in the form of sugars and starches, enables a flower to attain full maturity. When flowers and foliages are cut, photosynthesis – the process whereby plants generate their food – is interrupted. The energy reserves contained in the stems and foliage are not sufficient to mature flowers and open buds. To maximize flower life, therefore, nutrients must be added, compensating for the loss of the flowers' own food-making capacity. Although there are many home-made and semi-professional recipes and formulas, the thoroughly researched, scientifically proven pre-treatment and flower foods are by far the most dependable, and give the best results to the florist.

Pre-treatments are used when flowers are cut at the nursery, and nutrients are again supplied when they are conditioned by the florist. This chain continues when the purchaser uses flower food at home.

There are many excellent brands of proprietary flower food. Customers should also be encouraged to use these products as it has been proved that this continued care increases vase life.

The ingredients of flower food

What does flower food contain? Most have a high sugar content – up to 95 per cent – in the form of saccharose and glucose. This explains why lemonade or ordinary sugar have a beneficial effect. The sugar provides the energy that the flowers need if they are to attain full maturity, and it enables the buds of flowers such as freesias, gladioli and carnation sprays to develop into open flowers.

Unhappily, the sugar also provides the perfect conditions for bacteria and micro-organisms to grow and multiply very rapidly. Bacteria will reproduce in the water, on the cut stem ends, and on damaged cells. This, in turn, leads to unpleasant smells and to the blockage of the water-carrying cells.

A balanced amount of bactericide in the flower food will inhibit the growth of micro-organisms and protect the stem ends from blockage, but it will not eliminate bacteria, so it is essential that clean equipment and clean containers are always used. Gerberas are particularly sensitive to bacteria, and their containers must be kept scrupulously clean. Use either a proprietary bucket and vase cleaner or a teaspoon of bleach to one litre of water to clean all containers.

To delay the effects of ageing and to make the flowers less sensitive to the ageing hormone, an ethylene inhibitor is included in the nutrient. Ethylene gas speeds maturity, so it is important not to mix mature stock with fresh materials and to keep cut flowers in cool temperatures.

Either citric acid or an acidifier is another ingredient. This lowers the pH of the water, because cut materials prefer a slightly acid water, as this contains less oxygen than an alkaline water.

Another component of the flower food stabilizes the colours of certain flowers, so that they retain their natural colour instead of fading.

Available foods

Many brands of flower food are available, and there are also various dispensing systems. All are aimed at prolonging the vase life of cut flowers, and the final choice will depend on individual preference. Flower foods are also manufactured for specific types of cut materials. Shrub and bulb flowers can have their own food, and bouvardia often arrives with its own 'personal' sachet. A liquid food is the most recent method to become available in bulk form to florists. A dispensing pump makes it easy to measure the correct amount.

Another way of providing flowers with nutrients uses a label containing the additives. This is simply dropped into tepid water, which is mixed with sugar. With each method, it is essential that all the ingredients are measured accurately, following the producer's instructions, and mixed thoroughly.

Preparation

It is important to prepare the food correctly, using tepid water. Dispensing systems are available to florists. These regulate the proportion of nutrient to water, ensuring that the correct amount of flower food is used. Excessive dilution of the flower food will deprive cut materials of its beneficial effects. Use the solution once only, and do not mix old solutions with new. One point to remember is that flower food should not be used with metal containers, as a reaction can occur between the metal and the nutrients. This hinders the performance of the food and can corrode the metal. Some manufacturers specify that their foods should not be used with lead crystal containers.

General aftercare advice

Flower care is quite straightforward, provided these basic points are remembered: buy high quality flowers from a reliable supplier; use clean equipment; cut all stems with a sharp knife; use tepid water and a flower nutrient, and follow the correct cold storage procedures. Research into post-harvest care continues, alongside the development of new cultivars and improved methods of growing. Florists must keep informed of new techniques and methods of prolonging the life of cut flowers and foliages. Finally, consumer education will lead to longer lasting flowers. Aftercare advice and personal tips are generally welcomed by the public. All flowers, whether they take the form of a small bunch of daffodils or a large gift arrangement, should leave the shop with care instructions and flower food. The more customers see flowers as a 'good buy', the more flowers will become part of everybody's weekly shop.

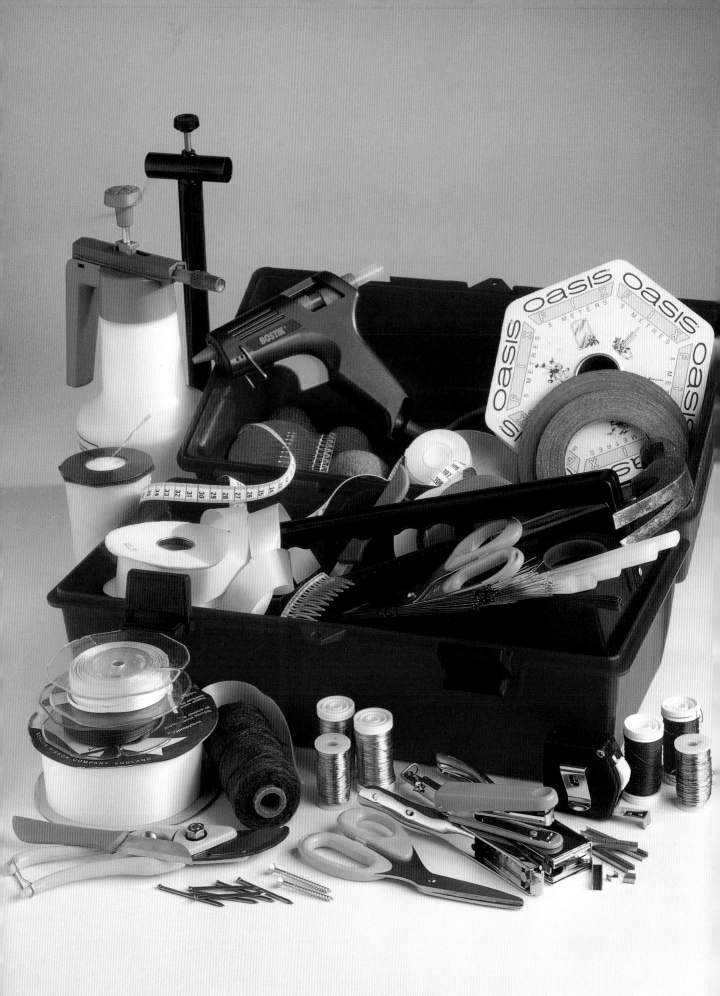

THE WORKBOX

A florist is a professionally-trained person and as such needs to look the part. Just as it is important to wear the correct clothes, makeup and hair style, it is also essential to have the correct equipment. A fashion designer or an artist could not do their job efficiently without specialist tools, and the same applies to the florist.

A plastic workbox is ideal for storing and carrying all the necessary equipment. It holds everything neatly in place, and is light and easy to take out on contracts. Included in this picture is a selection of tools and equipment necessary for work to be carried out efficiently.

CUTTING TOOLS, TAPES & WIRES

Cutting equipment

Certain pieces of equipment are essential while others are simply useful, so purchase the essential items at the start, adding the others when you can afford them. Always buy the correct tool for the job – with care and regular maintenance, your tools will last for years.

Florists' scissors You will need a pair that will cut both stems and wires and, when necessary, ribbons.

Sharp knives This is a must for cutting stems when conditioning flowers and for flower arranging. The small orange-handled fixed-blade knives are ideal, cheap, and easily obtained from wholesalers.

A long-bladed knife is very useful for cutting floral foam.

An electric carving knife is ideal for cutting shapes from foam designer sheets.

Secateurs These are excellent for cutting thick woody stems.

Florists' tape This is used to conceal wires and seal stem ends. There are two main types of tape – the first is plastic and stretches, the warmth of your hand helping to secure it. The second type resembles crêpe paper, but is usually slightly sticky.

The tapes are supplied in a variety of colours – green, brown, black, white and a range of pastel shades. Green is normally used with fresh materials, and brown with dried flowers.

Florists' wire This is used to support, control and anchor materials, lengthen stems and reduce weight. Always wire internally wherever possible, and use the finest gauge of wire that will give sufficient support.

The larger the number, the thicker the gauge of a stub wire, the most popular

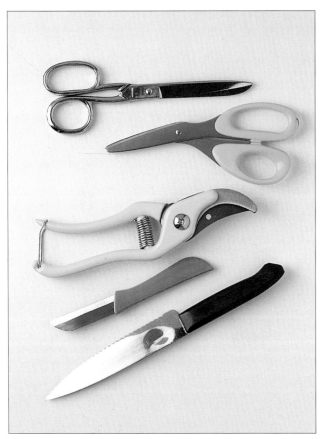

A selection of cutting tools is shown here – good quality equipment is essential and will last for many years.

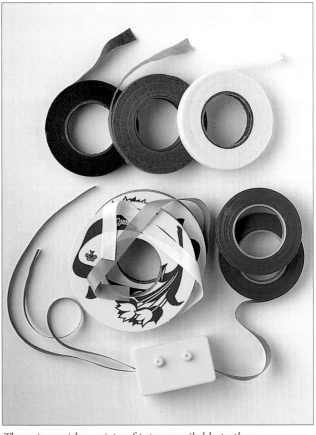

There is a wide variety of tapes available to the florist, and it is a matter of personal preference which is used.

gauges being as follows: 1.25mm (18g), 0.90mm (20g), 0.71mm (22g), 0.56mm (24g), 0.46mm (26g), 0.38mm (28g), 0.32mm (30g), 0.28mm (31g) and 0.24mm (32g).

Binding wire is also available in the following sizes: 0.56mm (24g) for binding moss on frames, and 0.32mm (30g) or 0.28mm (31g), in silver or green, for use in wedding work. Wholesalers can supply coloured binding wire for decorative work.

Wire storage Most florists store their wires in metal containers when using them in the work room. These are ideal as the heavy containers do not tip over and spill, and the different sizes of wire are stored separately while being easily accessible.

New packs of wire should always be kept in dry conditions, as the blue annealed type tend to rust, making them unpleasant to handle. It is possible to buy green-coated rustproof wires.

A metal wire stand is ideal for keeping wires tidy when in use in the work room. Stands can be made at home from metal tubes welded to a base.

Coloured decorative binding wires add a new dimension to this topiary tree. They are available in a medley of colours from wholesalers.

SAFETY WITH GLUE GUNS

The discussion of health and safety provisions has been linked here with information about glue guns and aerosols because the inappropriate use of these can prove extremely dangerous.

Health and safety regulations

Every country has laws governing the health and safety of staff and the public at a place of work, the chief of these in the United Kingdom being the Health and Safety at Work Act, 1974. Its requirements, which outline a sensible working practice for any floristry environment, stipulate that the employer shall provide 'so far as reasonably practical':

- A safe place of work;
- Safe systems of work;
- Safe access and egress (exit), and
- Equipment which is in a safe condition.

If there are more than five employees, they must be given a clearly written safety policy.

The employee is required to cooperate with the employer to enhance the safety of the place of work. This means that if safety equipment and a safe method of work is provided by the employer, the employee must use them, and if a fault is seen, this must be reported to the employer.

First aid box

Every place of work must have a first aid box, which must be easily accessible and should only contain items such as bandages, eye pads, plasters, saline and water-based wipes. Persons trained in First Aid are required 'as appropriate to the place of work and the work engaged in'.

An accident book is required to be kept, with notes on any accident, no matter how minor, together with the date it took place and the action taken. Required by law, this is a useful reference if problems arise.

The use of glue in floristry is increasing. Glue guns, using both hot and cool melts, glue pots into which stems can be dipped, and cold glues are all now employed by the florist, speeding the assembly of mechanics and securing materials – fresh, dried and artificial. It is advisable always to use the correct glue for the job. If you are uncertain, check with the manufacturer.

It is common sense to make sure that staff are always up-to-date with anti-tetanus injections, and particular care should be taken by anyone who may be allergic to certain materials.

Hazardous substances

All potentially hazardous substances must be handled with care, and in the United Kingdom 'The Control of Substances Hazardous to Health Regulations, 1988' requires employers to assess all substances at the place of work as to the hazard that such substances have by their nature. When a substance has been found to carry an unacceptable level of risk, the steps which will render it safe must then be recorded, and all staff are required to observe these safe practices.

Glue guns

Glue guns are a comparatively recent, but now important, development in the floristry industry, performing numerous tasks effortlessly and securely – for example, attaching foam to containers and wall swags, ribbon to foam bases, or flowers into bouquet holders.

Glue guns are divided into two types – hot and cool melt. The latter is ideal for attaching synthetic ribbons, which might otherwise melt, and the former is used for all other tasks.

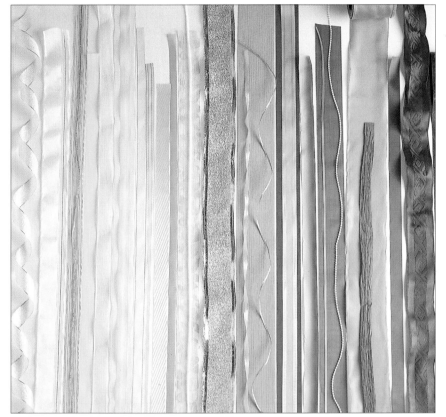

Ribbons form an intrinsic part of floristry and flower arranging. They can transform arrangements and enhance bouquets, adding a new dimension to both colour and texture. The ribbons displayed show a very small selection of the thousands available to florists. Most wholesalers have a good selection of basic ribbons, plus many more designed for particular occasions, such as Valentine's Day, Christmas or Mother's Day.

A vast range of aerosol paint colours and finishes is available to the florist. Provided simple safety rules are followed, spray painting is a straightforward and cost-effective way of giving a new look to dated containers and accessories. Basic, inexpensive items can be turned into stylish, modern containers and accessories at little cost. Individual and personalized effects can easily be created for distinctive designs or special occasions.

Glue pots are a more recent development, glue sticks being melted in a special heated pot, into which stems can be dipped.

Spray paints are available in a wide range of colours. They can safely be used on fresh and dried flowers, and containers and bases. Surface sealers, cleaners, flame retardants and leaf shine are also available in aerosol cans.

Glue gun and spray can safety rules

Glue guns, like aerosols, can be dangerous if used carelessly, and the following rules should always be applied.

- Never leave an unattended glue gun switched on.
- Electric cables should not be allowed to trail across the floor; there must be sufficient sockets along the work benches to avoid any need for extension cables.
- Never unblock the nozzle of a spray can with a pin or wire when the nozzle is still attached to the can.
- Never use spray cans or glue in an unventilated or poorly ventilated room.

FLOWER ARRANGING TOOLS

I t is vital to use the correct tools for any job, a rule that applies to flower arranging just as much as to any other branch of floristry. There is a vast array of containers, foam and tapes and the florist must select the correct items for each design.

The invention of floral foam about forty years ago brought about dramatic changes in the art of flower arranging. Until that time, flowers were arranged in wet sand, clay or chicken wire. The early types took forty minutes to soak, but today's wet foams only take one and a half minutes.

Bricks and cylinders Floral foam, which is available under many brand names, comes in several shapes, sizes and densities, variously designed to suit different containers and the weight of specific types of plant material. The best-known shapes are the bricks and cylinders.

Foam-filled trays Also available are foam-filled trays, ready-prepared for designs such as wall swags, marquee-pole arrangements and sympathy tributes. These can be found in biodegradable form. It is also possible to obtain long bars of foam covered in plastic film, and these are ideal either for large floral arrangements to be hung on walls or for casket sprays.

Some foam is treated with fire retardent, a valuable feature now that fire regulations have been tightened up. In addition, most

Flower arranging is a very important part of the floristry industry. Many companies are involved in manufacturing and supplying the tools and equipment specifically designed for this purpose, and it is impossible to show anything but a very small selection of the products on offer. The choice grows and improves daily as companies upgrade or build onto their already substantial ranges.

foam companies are showing concern to ensure that their products are environmentally friendly.

Containers An immense range of shapes, colours, sizes and types of container is on offer at each florists' wholesaler.

Many different plastic saucers and dishes have been designed to fit foam cylinders and blocks. They are cheap in price and are ideal for arrangements intended for those customers who prefer to spend their money on flowers rather than the container.

For those who are prepared to spend a little extra, there are the pottery or glass containers. These are very suitable for certain arrangements, such as continental designs, in which the container forms an integral part of the whole. They also have a place in novelty designs, such as new baby arrangements.

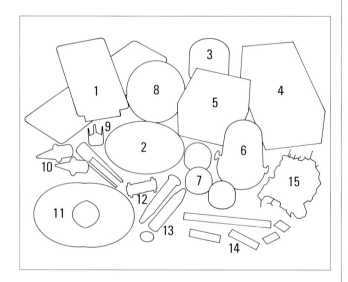

Key

1 Plastic trays
2 Cylinder saucer
3 Foam cylinder
4 Foam block
5 Plastic base containing caged foam
6 Plastic base with foam-suction attachment (Auto Corso)
7 Plastic base with

adhesive pad and wet and dry foam (Mini Deco)
8 Plastic dish
9 Plastic frog (pin holder)
10 Candle holders
11 Pot tape
12 Silver binding wire
13 Orchid tubes
14 Fix
15 Chicken wire

Pot tape This sticky tape, available in green and white, is used to secure floral foam into containers. It adheres very securely to itself.

Fix A non-setting adhesive, this comes on a roll. It can be cut into small pieces and is ideal for securing plastic frogs or candle cups into position.

Frogs These are plastic pin holders, used to secure floral foam into a container.

Candle holder These are used to secure candles into arrangements.

Chicken wire This still has a place in large arrangements, where it provides extra strengthening for floral foam, and it is sometimes used in large pots or vases, where it is crumpled up to hold stems in position.

Binding wire This is sometimes needed to secure the chicken wire in place.

Orchid tubes Plastic tubes are occasionally useful when only one flowering stem needs to be in water, for example a stem of orchids in a pot-et-fleur. The stem is pushed through the hole in the rubber cap, and the tube is placed in the compost.

Mister or sprayer This is essential for spraying a fine mist of water on arrangements to keep them fresh.

Dried or fabric arrangements

The stems of dried or fabric flowers are fine and hard and therefore need very little foam to secure them. The dry floral foam, which is normally coloured brown to avoid confusion with the wet variety, is specifically designed for this use. There is also a clay-type substance, which sets hard once an arrangement is complete.

Glue guns are very useful, as the foam can be glued into the container and, for added security in designs such as wall hangings, the stems can similarly be glued into the foam.

Covering the mechanics often presents problems in dried arrangements; lichen moss, hairpinned into position, frequently provides the ideal solution. If necessary, foam can be sprayed to match the design.

WEDDING EQUIPMENT

Wedding work has changed out of all recognition in the last few years. Until recently, all one needed to make a bouquet was a selection of wires and florists' tape. Each flower was wired individually before being bound into place. Because the flowers were wired, it was very easy to manipulate them into a definite shape, but unfortunately, it was also very easy to produce a rigid, stiff bouquet.

During the 1960s and 1970s, this was perhaps acceptable, as wedding bouquets were then small and formal. As the fashion in wedding dresses changed, however, so did the bouquets, becoming larger and more natural, especially after the wedding of Prince Charles and Lady Diana, in 1981.

Bouquet holders were developed to hold full stems of flower material, the idea being an adaptation of the old-fashioned moss balls used by Victorian gardeners to produce the huge bouquets of the past.

The bouquet holders are available in both wet and dry foam, and in several shapes and sizes. Stands are also available to hold them firmly in place while the bouquet is produced. Glue may be used to secure the stems firmly into position.

The wedding equipment industry also produces a selection of accessories, including headbands and combs onto which flowers may be glued, badges for corsages and buttonhole holders, plus dolly bags, baskets and hoops for bridesmaids to carry.

Design skill and artistic ability are still very necessary to a trained florist, but hopefully the new developments make work quicker and easier.

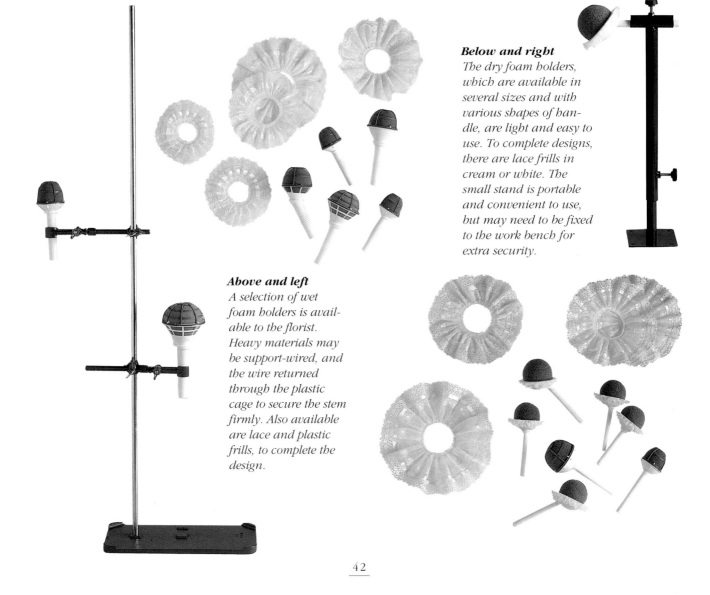

Below and right
The dry foam holders, which are available in several sizes and with various shapes of handle, are light and easy to use. To complete designs, there are lace frills in cream or white. The small stand is portable and convenient to use, but may need to be fixed to the work bench for extra security.

Above and left
A selection of wet foam holders is available to the florist. Heavy materials may be support-wired, and the wire returned through the plastic cage to secure the stem firmly. Also available are lace and plastic frills, to complete the design.

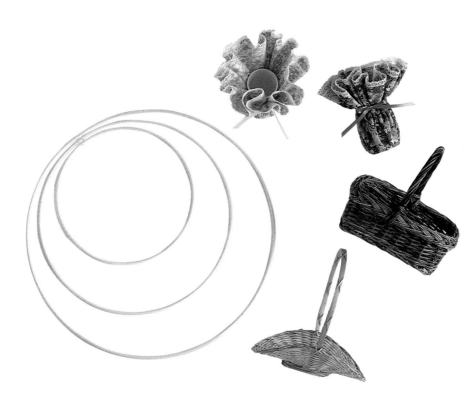

Left *Hoops became popular after the royal wedding of Prince Andrew and Sarah Ferguson. They may be bound in ribbon before being decorated with flowers. Baskets and dolly bags are also suitable for bridesmaids.*

Right *Millinery wire forms an ideal base for a traditional garland headdress. When cut, it can be shaped into a circle of the correct size and taped. The flowers are then taped onto the band. Another method is to glue the flowers on to a plastic foundation to form a circlet or an Alice band.*

Left *The small circle of foam forms an ideal base for a prayer book spray or cake top decoration. The base is sticky, and attaches itself firmly to any surface. Corsage badges and buttonhole holders make wiring unnecessary and preparation much quicker.*

FOAM FRAMES

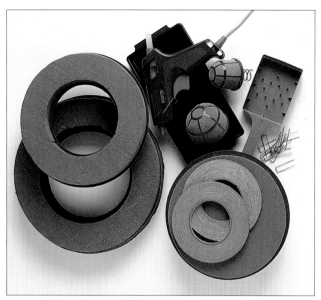

A selection of the foam wreaths and spray trays that have replaced traditional wire frames and moss in many shops.

F oam frames, which are much cleaner and quicker to use, and give a truly professional look to sympathy designs, have replaced moss in many florists' shops. They are made by several companies, but the technique and finished frames are similar in appearance.

The cheaper ranges are formed of wet foam, glued onto a non-absorbent backing, through which wires can be pushed if necessary. They come in a variety of basic shapes, including hearts, crosses, wreaths, chaplets, pillows and cushions, as well as the more unusual gates of heaven, teddy bears, letters of the alphabet, and numbers one to nine.

The more expensive types are set in moulded plastic frames, which retain the moisture and include a lip support for ribbon and foliage, as well as non-slip rubber feet. It is also possible to purchase a foam bump, which is a plastic cage, filled with wet foam, into which the spray is arranged.

Many people believe that flowers last longer in wet foam than in moss, and it is quicker to work with foam frames, which are pleasant and easy to handle.

The foam frames now available to the florist have speeded up sympathy work and made complex designs much easier to achieve.

Many unusual shapes have now been added to the range of foam frames, including teddy bears, anchors, guitars and open books.

TRADITIONAL FRAMES

Despite the advent of foam frames, many florists still prefer to keep to the traditional methods of making sympathy designs; they feel happier wiring all the flowers and securing them in moss.

The two types of frame require totally different skills. For a moss frame, sphagnum moss is bound to the wire frame with 0.56mm (24 gauge) binding wire. Normally, the frame is then backed with wreath wrap, which is a plastic strip, fastened to the back of the mossed frame with German pins. The backing gives the design a professional finish, and helps to retain moisture. Holly wreaths are also made by this method, as the finished design is very secure and can either hang on the front door or be placed on a grave.

When the frame has been backed, all flowers are then support wired, usually with 0.56mm or 0.71mm (24 or 22 gauge) green annealed stub wires. A 0.90mm (20 gauge) mount wire is wound around the base of the stem; this is then inserted into the moss. Woody-stemmed foliage only needs mount wires, as the stems require no extra support.

After a wire frame has been mossed, it is then backed, two methods being demonstrated here – a backing of plastic wreath wrap, and one of laurel leaves.

Above *In the picture is a selection of the wire frames now available from wholesalers. Also shown is sphagnum moss, wreath wrap, and laurel leaves, which are used to back the frames.*

Right *Although many unusual shapes of frame are now available in foam as well as wire, some designs may only be obtained as wire frames.*

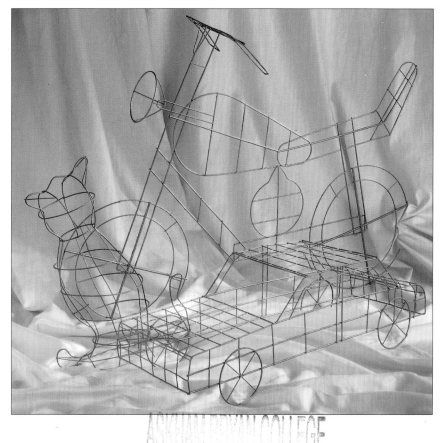

GIFT WRAPPING

Gift wrapping enhances the appearance of flowers as well as making them into a special and personal gift. It also protects them from the elements and from accidental damage, and slows down transpiration.

There are many ways of gift wrapping cut flowers – shop paper, cellophane on a roll, and cardboard and acetate boxes in a variety of shapes and sizes. When correctly wrapped, flowers are easy to carry and pleasant to handle.

Cone wrap A bunch of cut flowers is normally just wrapped in shop paper, but clear cellophane may be used as an alternative, and a suitable bow may be added to make a bunch even more attractive.

Cellophane or presentation bag These are still used by many shops, but the flat pack has been superseded in many areas by the all-round tied bunch.

Cellophane on a roll Fitted into a wall-hung dispenser with a cutting edge, providing accessibility and ease of usage, this makes an excellent covering for bouquets, arrangements and plants. Ribbon bows are normally added to complement the design. The shop's name or logo is usually printed across the cellophane.

Boxes For flowers that will be travelling any distance, cardboard boxes are a secure form of packing. Those with windows have the added benefit of displaying the flowers. Boxes can also be decorated with ribbons and bows to enhance the finish.

PVC cylinders and tubes Very popular for single flowers, stems of orchids and corsages, these come in a vast array of shapes and sizes, and are usually decorated with ribbons or bows, to complete the design.

Ribbon Gift wrapping makes any plant or bunch of flowers look festive, and a lavish bow adds the finishing touch.

Wedding flowers All wedding designs should be attractively packaged before delivery. Bridal boxes should be prepared well before the delivery date, and as soon as the bouquet is complete it should be packed in a box to keep it fresh. Store bridal arrangements in a cool area until delivery.

Gift cards Cards and envelopes should always be clearly and neatly written. The full name and address of the recipient should be printed on the envelope, together with any special delivery instructions.

Care cards Care cards or instructions on how to look after the flowers or plants should be attached to all deliveries.

The picture shows a small selection of materials available for gift-wrapping flowers or plants. Also shown are flowers in acetate containers and a corsage bag. Ribbons are used to enhance the designs, and form an intrinsic part of gift wrapping.

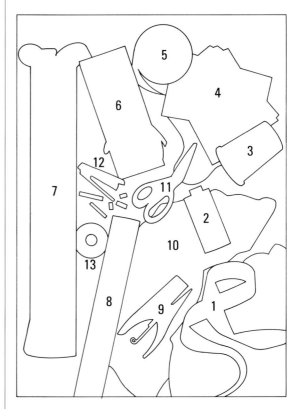

Key

1	Ribbon	8	Roll of cellophane
2	Twine	9	Stapler
3	Stem tie	10	Rondello (black
4	Corsage bag		cellophane)
5	Reel of ribbon	11	Scissors
6	Corsage box	12	Mini stapler
7	PVC tube	13	Stem tube

BASIC METHODS AND TECHNIQUES

The floristry industry has its own special techniques and skills, and it is essential that a good florist should possess the fundamental know-how to support and control all types of materials. A well-trained florist will produce designs that have a professional finish, achieved by discrete workmanship and well-concealed construction techniques. Only with practice, however tedious this may seem at times, can you acquire the necessary dexterity and expertise that will enable you to turn your creative ideas into successful finished designs.

An understanding of the technical language used in the shop or workroom is also important, as many specialist terms, such as box pleating, taping and spiralling, are used.

WIRING METHODS

S mall flower heads need to be supported and controlled when used in the traditional construction of corsages, buttonholes and headdresses. It would be convenient if there were just one basic wiring method, but unfortunately this is not so. The florist handles a wide range of materials requiring individual wiring methods. More wiring techniques are covered in lesson 7 (pages 140-179).

1 *Remove most of the stem to reduce bulk and weight, and select the appropriate wire – if it is too thick, the flower will be rigid; if it is too fine, it will give insufficient support.*

Singapore orchids

Handling the orchid with care, as petals are easily cracked or damaged, remove a flower head from the main stem, leaving only a small portion of stem. Insert a length of silver wire through the base of the flower, leaving one end longer than the other; bring the wire ends together, twisting the short end around both the stem and the longer end of wire, which is brought down to form an artificial stem. Neatly tape this stem.

Hyacinths

Bend a silver wire in half, twisting it to make a small loop. Gently remove a flower head, leaving a short stem. Insert the wire down and through the flower head, so the loop is hidden in the flower head. Complete as above.

Carnation spray

Leaving a small portion of stem, remove an individual flower from the spray. Make a small hook at the top of the wire and insert the wire through the head of the flower, pulling it carefully so that the hook is hidden in the flower centre. Start taping at the base of the stem.

Rose

Remove most of the stem; insert a stub wire up into the stem, pushing it securely into the seed box, then tape.

2 *Handling flowers carefully to avoid damaging fragile heads or stems, insert a wire into the stem and base of each flower, ensuring that the wire is secure and completely hidden.*

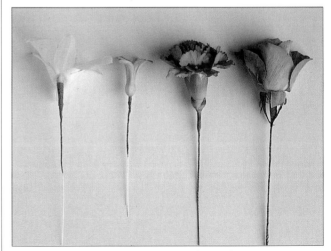

3 *When all the materials are wired, neatly tape each to form a natural-looking stem, using half-width tape for delicate materials. The materials are now prepared for use in designs.*

A single leg mount
Place a wire behind the (support-wired) rose, and bring both wires parallel; twist the longest wire around the stem and the other wire, bringing it down to form one stem. The foliage stems are formed in a fan and mounted in the same way.

Mounting

This is the method of attaching a wire to the base of the stem or stems of foliage or a support-wired flower, usually to give anchorage or additional support. The gauge of mount wire, which is generally heavier than that of the support wire, depends on the weight of the materials and their end use; for example, a piece of *Asparagus setaceus* to be used in a corsage would be mounted on a fine wire. Foliage for a wreath edging would require a heavier wire.

Single leg mount

This gives extra security, as a single wire can be pushed right through a foam or moss base and then returned back into the base. Use this technique to secure focal-point

A double leg mount
The rose is support-wired, and the foliage arranged in fans. Place a wire behind the materials; bring both prongs parallel to the stem; twist one prong around the stem and bring it back down – you now have a double leg mount.

flowers in funeral tributes and wedding bouquets and posies in foam holders (when a glue gun is not being used). For the single leg mount, one end of the wire (the left-hand side if you are right handed), should be considerably longer than the other, which is twisted around the stem.

Double leg mount

This can be used to anchor foliage into the base of a funeral wreath. It is formed in the same way as the above, except that the left-hand end of wire is just a little longer than the right-hand one, so that both finish equal in length, making a two-pronged mount. Both single and double leg mounts (when complete) form a wire loop at the back, giving extra support.

TAPING

This is the technique of covering wires with a specially manufactured tape. A good florist must be able to tape materials quickly and neatly, and in the beginning this will take practice. Wired stems are taped for the reasons given below.

● Taping conceals the wires, giving protection and a professional appearance that heightens the general public's appreciation of the florist's skills.

● Sealing the stem with tape gives a natural appearance and holds in the moisture, prolonging the life of the materials that can no longer take up water.

Method

Prepare the materials for taping. Hold the item to be taped in your left hand (if right-handed), between your thumb and forefinger, and the tape in your right hand, again between the thumb and forefinger (reverse the positions if you are left handed). Gently rotate the item, so that tape winds around the top of the stem, then stretch the tape against the stem, at a 45 degree angle.

Continue to rotate the item carefully, stretching the tape and at the same time moving down the support wire, ensuring that the tape covers the wire. Twist the tape onto itself to seal the end. The taping has now created the required natural stem-like appearance.

1 *Prepare your materials: remove most of the stem and then wire it, using the appropriate method and the correct gauge of wire.*

2 *Apply the tape firmly, sealing the lower end of the stem and covering the wire. Taping should look smooth, giving the appearance of being sprayed on.*

Units

Unit construction is the technique of securing several pieces of material to form one composite stem. There are three different types of unit: branching, ribbed, and natural.

Branching unit construction

First wire and tape single flowers or leaves. Starting with bud materials, firmly tape as shown, leaving space between the individual flowers or leaves to form a natural-looking component stem. These small units can be used in corsages, prayer book and hat sprays. For longer units, composite stems are taped onto a heavier support wire. These units can then be used in posies or bouquets.

It is important to use materials of a single type and colour, such as pink nerines, white hyacinths, a peach carnation spray or *Hedera helix* 'Glacier'. It is also important to grade materials, starting with a bud at the tip, and increasing in size as you work down the stem. Assembling the flowers and foliages into units will make the construction of a design quick and easy.

Ribbed unit construction

First prepare single flowers, leaves or ribbons. Small clusters of materials, such as berries or hydrangea florets, can also be wired together. Materials are then closely taped on a support wire, leaving no stems visible.

A ribbed unit can either be formed with materials of the same type and colour, or with a combination of flowers, foliage, berries and ribbons.

Materials can be graded in size, as for a branching unit. This ribbed construction is used in novelty designs, such as fans. It can, however, be made with materials of a similar size. Use this method for the garland or circlet headdress that is now fashionable for brides and bridesmaids.

Natural unit construction

Here, the materials – convallaria, muscari or ixia, for example – are left on the natural stem, and the stems are grouped and mounted for use in various types of wedding design. This type of unit is often used in European-style designs.

Branching unit

Wire and tape single leaves (use loop stitch, see page 145) or flowers. Tape the smallest leaf to a support wire; leave a space; tape a second leaf, and so on. Wires must be covered with tape.

Ribbed unit

Prepare materials, then tape a flower to the support wire; place a leaf close to it and tape. Add materials until the unit is the required length, then tape the stem.

Natural unit

Take several pieces of foliage or flowers and double leg mount. Tape and cover the mount and form the stem.

SUPPORT WIRING

Long-stemmed flowers may be wired to give support and control. Select a wire that gives support, but not rigidity, and where possible conceal wires internally. All support wires must finish at the stem end.

There are three basic forms of support wiring, the choice depending on the stem structure: internal wiring, for hollow stems; semi-internal, for soft stems, and external for woody/hard stems.

External method

Insert the wire (either taped or coated) into the flower base and twist it around the stem at regular intervals.

Semi-internal

Insert the (taped or coated) wire into the stem, 4-5cm (1½-2in) below the flower and push it up into the base. The protruding wire is twisted around the stem, avoiding the foliage.

Internal wiring

Make a small hook at one end of the wire. With the flower in your left hand (reverse if left-handed), insert the wire through the flower and down the stem, hiding the hook in the flower.

The long-stemmed flower is now ready to be used.

1 Wires are inserted into the carnation seed box, and below the tulip flower head. Push a hooked wire into the daffodil head. External and semi-internal wires should taped or coated.

2 For the carnation and tulip, the wire is carefully twisted around the stem at regular intervals, avoiding the foliage. The daffodil wire is completely hidden in the hollow stem

USING GLUE

Many florists now use glue instead of the traditional wire for securing flowers, foliage and ribbon into specially-prepared bases and holders.

Florists have the choice of using glue guns, pans, pots, tubes or aerosols. Each method has its own uses and advantages, but the gun is the most popular method of applying glue.

To use glue effectively, you must be able to work at speed and must know exactly where the materials are to be positioned. Hot melted glue must be used with care (see pages 38-9); always glue materials to dry foam, which can be moistened afterwards. With these provisos, glue can be used in many ways.

Wedding designs When using a foam holder (see page 162), add glue to the flower and foliage stems to give extra security. A headdress is quickly assembled by gluing fresh, fabric or artificial materials to a comb or plastic band (see page 160). For corsages, glue materials onto specially-designed corsage badges. Single or small sprays of flowers can be glued to the ribbon markers of a prayer book or ribbon streamers in a posy. Pearls or beads can look effective when glued into the centre of, for example, lilies.

Sympathy tributes Various edgings of lace, single leaves or ribbons can be glued to foam frames. For extra security, glue the foam base for the spray or cluster to the frame. Glue into position the flowers or leaves used to cover the base and the materials for the spray/cluster – once again, this gives extra security.

Dried, fabric or artificial materials For a flower arrangement, glue the dry foam onto your chosen container, then secure your selected materials with glue. Pictures, garlands and swags can all be quickly assembled by gluing an attractive combination of materials to a frame or base.

Hot glue tip A petal of your last 'Casablanca' lily has broken off. Do not panic. Ensuring both are dry, carefully put a line of glue on the main flower and petal. Replace the petal and hold until the glue has dried.

For a corsage made on a badge, select good quality, well-conditioned materials. Glue the outline materials in place first, then add filler flowers and leaves, finishing with the main flower.

To prepare a ribbon edging, put a band of glue, about 15cm (6in) long, along the lip of the frame. Place the ribbon on the glue and press it firmly in place; continue until the frame is complete.

BOWS

Making a bow is one of the first skills that a florist must acquire. There are various techniques, each giving a different finished result. Perfect bow-making requires practice, but once perfected, your skill will often be admired by customers, especially if you make bows in the shop, where they can see and appreciate your artistry. A pretty ribbon bow will often be kept by the customer as a memento of a special flower gift.

A well-made bow has many uses: it can complete the gift-wrapping of flowers; it may add an attractive finish to a hand-tied bouquet or flower arrangement, or lend a touch of glamour to a door garland.

Polypropylene (or Polytie) ribbon bows are mostly used in funeral tributes, as this type of ribbon does not absorb water. The more expensive satins, velvets and lacy ribbon bows are added to corsages, headdresses, posies and bouquets, and a ribbon bow is attached to the handle of the bridal bouquet to give an attractive finish.

Bows can be large and bold or small and dainty, depending on the width of ribbon. A single bow is made with one type of ribbon, but a double bow may combine two types or colours of ribbon. A completed bow may have two, four, six, eight or even more loops, depending on its use.

For the peak selling periods of Christmas, Valentine's Day and Mother's Day, bows should be prepared during a quiet time in the shop, colour coded and stored in polythene bags until required.

The figure-of-eight method

There are many different methods of making a bow, but one of the most versatile is the figure-of-eight technique. To make this type of bow, cut a length of ribbon and hold it firmly between the thumb and forefinger of your left hand (reverse positions if you are left handed), with a short length forming the streamer. Fold the ribbon back and gather it with your thumb and forefinger, forming a loop, then repeat to make the second loop. Make two further loops, checking that all are the same size, and secure all the loops together, either by binding a taped wire at the centre, or by tying them with a length of similar, but narrow, ribbon.

Neatly trim the streamers and open out the loops; the bow is now ready for use.

1 *Cut a length of ribbon. Use one end to form a short streamer, and make two loops, checking that both are the same size.*

2 *Repeat the process, making four loops and two streamers. The ribbon loops should meet and cross at a central point.*

3 *Gather the ribbon at the cross-over point and secure it with a taped wire or a narrow length of similar ribbon.*

Large or small, bold or dainty, single or double, and made in a range of florists' ribbons – there is a bow for almost every type of design.

PRINCIPLES

The principles of design are the guidelines which help in the selection and use of flowers, foliage, bases, containers and accessories, and enable the florist to produce an aesthetically pleasing design. It is essential to know how to appreciate and apply these basic principles of design, scale and proportion, balance and harmony. All of these are used in conjunction with the further elements of rhythm, space, texture and, of course, colour.

Colour is a very important component of any design, having its own structure and language. An understanding of the colour wheel and how colours relate to each other is invaluable. The ability to choose an attractive colour combination and then to use it skilfully will lift an ordinary design, whether it is a handtied posy, bouquet, arrangement or tribute, turning it into something that is beautiful, distinctive and memorable.

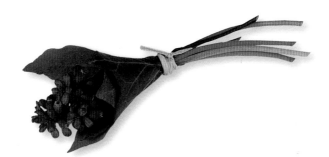

COLOUR

W hat is colour? A basic explanation is that colour is experienced when a beam of light is refracted (broken) by a surface, and the eye then transmits the effect to the brain; in other words, we can say that it is essentially a visual sensation.

The colour wheel

For practical use in floristry, it is best to refer to a wheel or triangle of 12 full strength hues (or colours), devised to illustrate the natural associations between colours. There are three so-called primary colours – red, yellow and blue. Any two of these, mixed together, produces a secondary colour; again, there are three secondaries – yellow and blue make green, yellow and red make orange, and red and blue make violet. The tertiary colours are produced by mixing a primary with an adjacent secondary colour; for example, blue and green make blue-green.

Achromatic or neutral colours – white, grey and black – are not technically colours (being colourless), but they are used to change the value of a hue; adding white, grey or black produces, respectively, a tint, tone or shade.

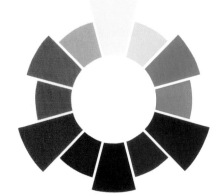

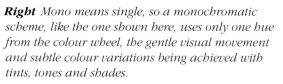

Right *Mono means single, so a monochromatic scheme, like the one shown here, uses only one hue from the colour wheel, the gentle visual movement and subtle colour variations being achieved with tints, tones and shades.*

Left *Recognized colour combinations incorporating a range of colours and their tints, tones and shades are called colour harmonies. The combination seen here is analogous. Analogous means similar, and this harmony incorporates adjacent colours – red, red-violet and violet – but includes only one primary, plus tints, tones and shades. Harmonies of this type produce rich, coordinated schemes.*

Far left *The value of one pure colour is changed by the addition of white (making a tint), grey (tone) or black (shade). Here, the red in the centre is at full strength. Small amounts of white in the flowers below make them lighter – a rosy pink, lighter still – pale pink, and finally a white with just a hint of pink. The addition of grey produces the crimson tone. With black, the colour becomes darker, burgundy being a shade of red.*

COLOUR HARMONIES

Colour, although we may not always acknowledge this, plays an important part in our lives, but whereas we may spend a considerable time coordinating the colours in our living rooms and bedrooms, we tend to think that all flowers will go together.

The effect of colour can be noted by florists, as flowers are often used to help to create an atmosphere or mood. Red is an exciting and warm colour; it can also be aggressive. Blue is almost the opposite, being cool and quiet. Violet is rich and sombre in some surroundings, while yellow is cheerful and warm. Orange is also warm and hospitable; green can be refreshing, and dark green is relaxing. Green, in any case, is the natural accompaniment to most flowers.

Colours are never seen in isolation in normal life; there are always surrounding colours, and they react with each other, for lighter or darker, for louder or quieter, for better or worse.

The way in which articifial light affects flower colours is important to florists. White fluorescent light makes blue look brighter, while ordinary light bulbs turn it to a rather depressing purplish grey. White, pink and orange look reasonably good in artificial light. Each time you decorate a marquee, take notes on the effect of diffused light on the flowers, as it is difficult to remember such details in the mind's eye.

When designing, use flowers with strong hues and bright colours towards the centre, and paler tints and tones at the outer edges. This will give visual stability as well as impact. A gentle gradation of colour is a subtle way of leading the eye into and through the design.

A colour wheel (see page 60) is a good aid to heighten your awareness of colour. If you have only thought about colour in general terms, a wheel will increase your confidence in using colour. Successful colour harmonies give assurance, and can lead to more complex and challenging ways of using colour in flower designs.

Split complementary
The blue hydrangeas, on one side of the colour circle, are put here, not with their direct opposite, which is orange, but with the colours lying on each side of orange – red-orange montbretias, and yellow-orange lilies and gerberas.

Contrast
Yellow and blue have no relationship with each other on the colour wheel, yet the two primaries produce a classic and satisfying colour combination in this pretty headdress.

Complementary

*Tints, tones and shades of blue
and orange are used in this
complementary colour harmony.
Aconitum, lavender and
hydrangeas contrast with the
pale tints of orange kniphofia
and roses.*

Near complementary

*Red roses and scarlet carnations
blend with blue-green pine and cedar
to make a near complementary
Christmas arrangement.*

Polychromatic

*A polychromatic colour harmony,
using many colours and many
flowers, brings Flemish and Dutch
painters to mind. This impressive type
of scheme can be difficult to blend well.*

THE USE OF COLOUR

It is the colour of flowers that first attracts the eye. Just think how often you have walked into a florist's shop and thought 'Aren't those deep red roses gorgeous!', or wandered through a friend's garden and gasped at the golden roses tumbling over the wall.

Flowers in their natural settings never clash; they always have foliage to soften the edges and merge the images. When we cut flowers and bring them into the house, however, we alter the setting by changing the lighting and background.

In the previous pages we have seen how the colour wheel is formed and how certain colours link to form colour harmonies. We now need to look at the individual colours and see how we can use their particular qualities to the greatest effect.

Movement
Colours can give a sensation of movement in a design. Reds, yellows and oranges can seem much nearer than blue and violet. This is important when placing an arrangement in a large building, where it might recede into the distance. Orange, red and yellow are known as advancing colours, while blue and purple are receding, and green is neutral and stable.

Warm and cold colours
Experiments have shown that people sitting in a blue room feel colder than they would in the same room, at the same temperature, when painted red or orange. It is thought that the brain associates blue with the cold sea and orange with the sun. In summer, an arrangement of blues and white, including delphiniums, larkspur, nigella, peonies and hydrangeas, is refreshing on a hot day. At Christmas, a huge log basket filled with red poinsettias looks cosy and inviting sitting in the hearth.

Luminosity
Some colours show up far more than others. White is the most dominant. Notice how white snow on a mountain top shows up from miles away, or white daisies in the garden seem to glow at dusk, when everything else has faded. Yellow is the most luminous chromatic colour, and violet the least. Again, this is important when placing flowers in a large church or hall, where the lighting may not be very good.

Feelings
Colours evoke feelings in people:
    Red – fire and passion;
    Yellow – spring cheerfulness;
    Blue – peace and tranquillity;
    Orange – autumnal warmth;
    Green – woodlands and growth;
    Violet – richness and splendour;
    Black – depression and death;
    White – chastity and purity.
The above generalizations are not hard-and-fast rules, but they do apply to most people, most of the time. White lilies are often used in church as a sign of purity. Red roses at Valentine's Day symbolize passion and love. Orange chrysanthemums and dahlias at harvest time signify autumn; red and orange provide warmth and excitement on a cold, frosty Hallowe'en night.

Backgrounds
Flower arrangements are always seen against a background. It may be the sitting room wallpaper or the grey stone of a church wall. When choosing wallpaper, we always look to see if it will go with the carpet, for we know by experience that it might look perfect in the shop, but dreadful when we get home. In the same way, the eye registers the difference, or contrast, between an arrangement and its background, so the former must be brighter than the latter, to enable it to show up.

The background to an arrangement is already in situ, so we need to create a design that will be seen against it. This is quite easy in large buildings, such as churches, where the walls are of grey stone or white paint. It becomes difficult if the walls are brightly coloured or painted. In this case, try to find an alternative site for the arrangement. If this is not possible, use a colour that will contrast with the background. If the red arrangement in the picture were to be placed against a red background, the two would blend into each other. Here, although the design is set against a bright colour, it stands out because the colour is blue, a receding colour. In every design, we tend automatically to use these principles, even when we do not, or cannot, give them their correct names.

*This dramatic and
modern arrangement
uses a bold combination
of the complementary
colours of blue and
orange to create an
immediate visual
impact. Colour balance
is achieved with the
integration of container,
flowers, foliage and
accessories.*

BASIC DESIGN PRINCIPLES

The outline of a symmetrical triangular arrangement is established. The height is the initial placement, the width and depth placements being added next. Groupings of spiky materials strengthen the outline.

The outline structures of the clusters on the wreath are created with various materials. Contorted willow gives direct lines; softer outlines are formed by montbretia and cotoneaster. The tips almost touch, giving visual movement.

D esigning is the skill of combining the various components, which in terms of floristry might include flowers, foliage, accessories, bases and/or containers, of a piece of work to produce a harmonious display, appropriate for a given occasion, event or setting.

There are various methods of designing. For instance, a design planned to the last detail and placement will tend to be static and rigid. On the other hand, allowing a design to evolve as one works can be a time-consuming process, and not really suitable for a busy florist. A good design will incorporate both approaches – a certain degree of planning and organization, to give order, plus experimentation, to provide individuality and originality.

Design can be divided into four major areas – form, lines/patterns, focal point and recession. The four basic principles are: **design**, **scale and proportion**, **balance** and **harmony**.

Form

Form includes the outline of any design, which can be either geometric or free form. Shape is sometimes used to describe the overall outline, but the former is two-dimensional, consisting of only height and width, and this creates a flat, boring design. Form should include not only height and width but also the important dimension of depth, and all floristry designs are three-dimensional.

Most forms of plant materials can be divided into three distinct groups and each group has an important part to play in a design: spike forms are used to establish the outline; mass forms are bold or interesting materials which can be used to create the focal line and area, and transitional forms are smaller sprays of flowers or foliage, which fill in the design.

Focal point and line

Area of dominance, accent point, centre of interest – these are just some of the design

A traditional focal point line is created by placing a series of graded sizes of flowers of one type and colour to form a gentle curve. The main focal flower is placed in a raised position, creating the elevated profile.

Different focal flowers are used to give each cluster interest. Only three anthuriums are used, because of their size and colour. Seven mini gerberas are incorporated to counterbalance the visual weight of the other flowers.

terms used to describe areas of emphasis and interest. The focal point and line exist for the following reasons:

• To attract and stimulate interest, the main focal point catching the eye and leading it into and through the design;
• To give emphasis and provide a strong visual line;
• To provide a sense of order and coordinate all materials within the completed design, as all lines and groupings should radiate from this;
• To avoid monotony, through its bold form, colour and large size.

Achieving a focal area

There are several ways of achieving a focal area.

• *Form* – select materials, such as lilies or gerberas, which are either round or have an interesting form, as this will attract and stimulate the eye.

• *Lines* – the main focal point is the most dominant line, formed by using 3, 5, 7 or more flowers (even numbers may also be used) to form a direct line. A graded line of flowers avoids the obvious 'bull's eye' focal point. All secondary lines must appear to radiate from or converge at this point.
• *Repetition* – use the same form and colour of one type of flower, in varying sizes, to create the main line.
• *Gradation* – buds are placed at the outer edge, then come the semi-open flowers, and larger materials are placed at the centre.
• *Colour* – full hues are used at the centre to attract the eye; paler colours are placed to the outside, where the design must appear lighter and have less visual attraction.
• *Grouping and recession* – a grouping of flowers or leaves, recessed at the focal area, will strengthen the visual depth of the design.
• *Contrast* – greater emphasis can be achieved by contrasting the forms, colours and texture at the main focal area.

LINES, GROUPINGS AND RECESSION

The strong, contrasting forms of spike and mass are now linked by graded sequences of flowers and foliage, placed in diagonal lines. Colours are carefully grouped to create visual balance.

Using a range of smaller flowers of blending colours, the outline of each separate spray is strengthened, and the centre of the design is filled in by placing materials on various levels.

L ines are visual paths, created by flowers, foliage or accessories, which the eye follows so they appear to have visual movement, which is called *rhythm*. The lines may be straight, curving, simple, bold or gentle; they may have vertical, horizontal or diagonal movement, and the visual effect of this can be fast or slow.

Ways of creating lines

Indirect lines are formed by a graded sequence of flowers, foliage types or accessories, and a line of this type is built up by placing materials on different levels, usually in vertical or diagonal lines. Horizontal lines should be avoided, as they tend to cut a design in half visually. Indirect lines link the outline and focal point line, and also fill in gaps, so that the design looks attractive from all angles.

A *direct line* appears where the line is visually solid. Materials that can be used to create a direct line include contorted willow (curving lines), *Phormium tenax* (straight lines), and trails of hedera or paper ribbon tubing.

Design lines

The main lines in a traditional design include the *outline*, which refers to the contours, and is created with spike materials; the *focal point line*, which is the main line of graded flowers, forming the centre of interest, and for which a mass form is used, and the *transitional lines*, which link the two contrasting spike and mass forms. Smaller materials are arranged in sequences (lines) of graded sizes, buds being placed towards the outer edge, and fuller flowers at the centre. Other materials can then be placed at various levels to fill in the gaps in the design.

The darker red shade of the Acer palmatum atrop-urpureum *foliage is recessed on various levels under the main focal point, giving visual depth and hiding the mechanics.*

The green gaultheria leaves provide a complementary colour link with the anthuriums. The acer foliage gives depth of colour, and the bold form of the geranium is a strong contrast with the lilies.

Recession

This is the placement of flowers, foliage and perhaps ribbon bows on *lower levels* within a design. To achieve recession, set back short-stemmed flowers, foliage or ribbons by placing them behind other materials.

A design that lacks recession will appear flat and two-dimensional, whereas materials placed on lower levels attract and lead the eye into the design, creating visual balance. Short-stemmed materials also have the advantage of hiding the mechanics, giving the design an attractive finish while strengthening the profile.

Achieving recession

- Use open flowers (avoid buds) and bold foliage, which will fill in the design quickly.
- Use darker colours – their recessive quality will give greater visual depth.
- Remember to leave space around the materials, otherwise the design will appear packed and visually bottom-heavy.

Other design terms

Finish All mechanics must be neatly hidden, so that the design looks attractive from all angles, including the back.

Economy This means using every flower, piece of foliage, ribbon bow or accessory to its full advantage, so that maximum use and value is gained.

Impact This is an instant visual impression, a special quality which demands instant attention. It is created by a striking colour scheme, good design skills, and the clever use of materials.

Distinction This is seen when everyday and extraordinary materials are used in an ingenious way, creating an unusual or special effect, but the design must always be appropriate for its given purpose.

RHYTHM

A wedding bouquet is often described as having a flowing line, or an arrangement will receive compliments for its strong visual movement. Both are working floristry terms, used to describe rhythm.

Rhythm is a dynamic element, bringing life to a design, and preventing it from becoming static and monotonous. A sense of rhythm is built up as the design is being made, and cannot be added later. This visual movement can be created in various ways.

Repetition – if certain features, such as line, size, form and colour, are repeated, the eye is stimulated and moves through the design.

Transition or gradation – of size, form and colour, imparts an orderly, measured sequence of change, creating an easy, gentle rhythm.

Space – in tradition designs, space between flowers and foliage stems is allowed in measured amounts, creating gentle, flowing lines. Line designs require larger or irregular areas of space to produce fast and visually strong movement.

Radiation – of lines, or groupings of lines that appear to radiate from or converge at one point.

Recession – placing darker short-stemmed materials on lower levels creates greater visual depth.

Direct line – some materials, such as contorted willow, attract the eye immediately and create spontaneous rhythm.

Above *Flowers and forms create visual movement. Transitional, smaller sprays link the two contrasts of spike and mass (see page 68) to create rhythm.*

Top right *Strong colours are used at the centre to create visual movement.*
Right *Gradation of size and form, artificially or naturally, creates rhythm.*

The swirling movements of flowers and foliage in this distinctive design emphasize the central area of interest. Curving and looped materials lead the eye around the sweeping lines of the arrangement.

SCALE

Scale, in floristry, is the relationships in size between flowers and flowers, flowers and foliage, and both of these and containers. Good scale is achieved when the relationships between all these components are pleasing. Scale and proportion are inter-linked, and sometimes there is confusion between the two. The relationship of individual flowers to each other and the container is scale; the balance between the flower materials and the container is proportion.

It is vital for any florist to recognize the importance of scale and proportion in design work. Whatever flowers or foliage are used, they must be in scale with each other, and the proportional balance between the arrangement and the container must also be correct. A design to be worn or carried must be in proportion to the person for whom it is made, and the flowers must also be in scale with the size of the design.

A corsage, hat or handbag spray

This is normally a small design, made to be either worn or carried at a wedding. The flower materials chosen must be small and dainty, and the flowers and foliage in scale with one another as well as with the bag or hat. Suitable flowers and foliage for this type of design include cymbidium orchids, spray carnations, roses, Singapore orchids, freesias and hedera leaves.

Wedding bouquets

Wedding bouquets can vary enormously in size, ranging from the small handtied posy that might be carried by the mature bride at a registry office to the magnificent bouquet carried by Princess Diana at her wedding at St Paul's cathedral. In both designs, the relationship between the individual flowers is important; they must be graded to form visual links, one to another.

In the handtied posy, it would be visually inappropriate to use spray carnations, freesias and spray roses, and then add fatsia leaves. The leaves would dominate the whole design, making it seem unbalanced and out of scale.

Princess Diana's bouquet used flowers of similar size, such as gardenias, convallaria, stephanotis, roses, and hedera leaves, but because these were used in large quantities, a bouquet some 1.35m (54in) in length was created. This was in proportion to the height of the bride, the volume of her dress, and the magnificence of the cathedral.

Churches and large buildings

Scale becomes very important when decorating large buildings. How often one sees a pedestal stand in a cathedral with a few small flowers placed in it. The flowers are out of scale with the large stand and the design is lost in the enormous building.

The scale of the bands of hydrangeas and moss causes confusion in this design, and the roses, spray carnations and leaves are too close in size for the spray to be in scale. Every item remains a component part, with no sense of the whole.

Right *Altering the width, and angle, of the hydrangea bands improves the visual image of the cross. The addition of smaller buds of spray carnation and cornflowers improves the scale. The roses now act as a focal point, and the design has unity.*

PROPORTION

As with the other design principles, an understanding of proportion will help a florist when designing a corsage, arrangement, bouquet or sympathy tribute.

In floristry terms, proportion is the amount or quantity of flower and foliage materials used in a design. The correct proportions of materials can be seen in the wedding bouquet in the main picture. In the design below, there are too many dendrobium orchids in the tail of the design in proportion to the quantity of flowers in the body of the bouquet.

This bouquet, with its attractive flowers, is not completely successful. Look carefully, and it can be seen that the proportions within the four key areas are not quite correct.

Colour

Proportion can also relate to the amount of colour, texture and space used within a design. The less effective design does not have enough of ribbon fern, the green pteris foliage, in proportion to the white flowers. A guide to the amount of colour that can be used within a successful design is 50–75 per cent of tints, 15–30 per cent of tones and shades, and just 10–20 per cent of strong hues. These proportions of colours, if used effectively, will give a pleasing design.

Texture

This is also lacking in the unsuccessful bouquet, many of the materials sharing a very similar visual quality. Texture is provided in the main picture by the buds of the larkspur and also by using more of the dendrobium spikes. There are no fixed measures for the amount of texture or space that is used within a design; both largely depend on the nature of the cut materials, containers, surroundings and positioning.

Overall proportions

The overall dimensions or measurements of height, width and depth must relate to one another and to the container in the correct proportions to create visual balance in a design. As floristry is an art form, there are only a few guidelines on proportion, and these are mainly for flower arrangements. For many designs, florists use the approximate proportions of one third to two thirds, and in the bouquet on the left we can see that the dimensions are not quite correct, the top of the design being rather short and cut off.

Proportion has a close relationship with scale, and therefore its surroundings and positioning will have an effect on proportion and the way in which it is used within a design. A good grasp of design and design principles is required of a florist – a rather daunting prospect for a new student. Design skills require practice with a broad range of flowers, foliage types, accessories and occasions, and these skills are not acquired quickly, partly due to seasonal restrictions.

Right *Within this design, there are good proportions of flowers and foliage, colouring and texture. The dimensions are visually balanced and pleasing to the eye.*

BALANCE

The Society of Floristry definition states that balance is 'the use of floral materials, foliage and colour so as to achieve both an actual and visual effect of structural strength and stability'. As this implies, there are two kinds of balance – actual and visual. Size graduation and the grouping of materials will achieve actual balance, with graduation and the grouping of colours added to achieve visual balance.

Actual balance

This is acquired by technical skill or getting the mechanics right. The arrangement should stand upright and not fall over backwards, forwards or sideways. It should be steady and sit comfortably. If a wedding bouquet is balanced, it should sit on the hand without being held. This means that it will be very comfortable to carry, and the bride will not have to worry about it tipping out of her hand. In the same manner, a corsage should sit flat when worn, or a handbag spray may sit on a handbag. This requires an even weight distribution, but not always a balance between equal numbers of flowers – two smaller flowers will counterbalance one large one.

The above arrangement has many design faults which upset the balance. These include the use of pale small flowers and foliage at the centre of the picture, dark flowers around the edges, and large leaves grouped to one side. Flowers are tightly clumped together.

Visual balance

As well as being actually balanced, the arrangement or bouquet should also be visually balanced. This is far more difficult to achieve. To be visually balanced, a design should have the following:
● A focal point or point of origin from which all stems appear to radiate;
● Darker colours to the centre of the design, and paler colours at the outer edges;
● Finer materials, such as spike ferns, used at the outer edges, and larger, more solid forms in the centre;
● Some materials recessed to give weight to the centre of the design.

Symmetrical balance

An arrangement may appear balanced because the left-hand side appears to be a mirror image of the right. A good example of this is the symmetrical triangle arrangement. In this, all the flowers and foliage are the same on each side, just like a pair of book ends or candlesticks sitting on the mantelpiece. The two sides balance because they are identical.

Asymmetrical balance

In an asymmetrical triangle arrangement, the two sides are not identical. If a line were drawn down the centre, one side would appear longer than the other. Here, the balance is achieved by using finer, thinner flowers on the long side, and bigger, bolder flowers on the short side. In this way, the two sides appear balanced, although they are not identical.

To test the finished design, draw an imaginary line down through the axis of the arrangement. The arrangement should appear to be visually balanced on either side of the line.

More design skill is needed to construct an asymmetrical arrangement, but this comes with experience and time.

Colour

Good use of colour is also important in achieving visual balance, and is an essential component of a pleasing design. More depth of colour is used in the centre of the design, again to give it visual weight, and the paler lighter colours are taken to the outer edges of the design.

Similar flowers have been used to achieve a much more pleasing design. The spike materials have been placed at the outer edges, establishing a stable outline. The larger pink flowers at the centre form a strong focal line. The other materials are now integrated.

HARMONY

An arrangement of parts into an agreeable and consistent whole is the dictionary definition of harmony. With flowers, one might imagine that it would always be easy to create a pleasing picture. As you can see here, however, not only can a combination of flowers be discordant, but the background plays a significant part in the harmony, or lack of it, of the design as a whole. Harmony is achieved when everything works well together.

Types of harmony

There are different types of harmony. Functional harmony, for example, is the

Above *The large and visually unbalanced corsage on this patterned background needs to have a greater overall harmony if it is to compete. Four different flowers, plus a not-quite-matching ribbon, result in a design that is as busy as the fabric.*

association between dissimilar objects that are commonly associated, such as a knife and fork.

The association between the poppy and laurel leaves is a symbolic harmony, like that between the dove and the olive branch.

In floristry, we can use seasonal harmony: autumn is associated with berries, wheat and with yellows and golds; spring evokes fresh new growth, daffodils and primroses.

In addition, a harmonious relationship should exist between the parts of the design, the container, plant materials and accessories; if the total appearance of a design gives an impression of unity, the result will be a harmonious picture.

The occasion will also dictate the choice of cut materials and accessories. A special party calls for flowers that can reflect and enhance the atmosphere. Bright, strong colours, and perhaps the addition of some balloons, would give an immediate effect to any room. Flowers for hotels and restaurants should blend with the decor and with the furnishings. Fashion should also be considered – a Victorian-style dress would be complemented by a Victorian posy.

Harmony and disharmony

In the designs shown here, we see how harmony can be achieved. The design on the left has no harmony of parts, having four different flowers and not even foliage to unite them. The design is as busy as the background, and the ribbon almost, but not quite, matches, therefore jarring slightly.

With a fabric as patterned as this, it can be advantageous to ask about accessories that are to be carried or worn. It may be possible to put flowers on a plainer background.

The flowers and foliage in the main design contrast yet harmonize, both within the design itself and in relation to the outfit and accessories. The colour of the corsage is sufficiently strong to stand out against the strong pattern, and is a little more subtle than the bright yellow rose.

Right *This specially designed handbag corsage is harmonious within itself and in relation to the outfit and accessories. The 'Jacaranda' roses, triteleia and lavender have been designed, together with the foliage, to create total harmony.*

TEXTURE

This is the tactile quality of an object. All objects possess a texture, and it is important to understand this quality and to use it well.

Used with skill in an arrangement, texture will add an extra dimension to the finished design. We want to touch the flowers to feel the velvety texture of rose petals or the waxy quality of an anthurium, but some textures we can feel without touching – rose petals are pleasant to touch, but we know in advance that they will feel velvety, or a pine cone will feel rough. It is the texural appearance of plant materials that is important, not the actual feel. Normally, we do not touch arrangements, but simply view them. Plant material can be categorized into many different textures, including the following:

velvety – silky
fluffy – hairy
woody – crinkled
leathery – dimpled
glossy – smooth

The use of texture

It is not enough simply to see different textures and understand that they exist. It is necessary to be able to group them in order to achieve impact and variety.

A design made entirely with shiny materials would be too dominant, the shiny surfaces would attract the eye by reflecting light, but the lack of contrast would make the design uninteresting.

Notice how dried arrangements are sometimes dull because the textures, and often the shapes, are similar. To overcome this, it is often a good idea to use a container, such as a basket with a shiny surface, that contrasts texturally with the flowers. The basket will then reflect the light and lift the arrangement. The role played by texture will vary according to the type of arrangement, in a monochromatic design, for example, where there is comparatively little colour variation, texture becomes a correspondingly important factor This consideration also applies to modern arrangements, where more importance is given to individual flowers or leaves than in a massed design.

The use of containers

Shiny textures always attract the eye far more than dull ones. When using containers such as brass, copper or glass, it is important to understand this, and to make the arrangement a bold one, that will draw the eye and also complement the container.

It is by using a balance of textures that one achieves interest. Too little contrast, and the design is boring; too much, and it becomes confusing.

A basic wall swag design has been made from fresh materials. The design lacks interest because it has no textural variation, the lilies and leaves both having the same shiny texture.

Right *The same design has been brought to life with the addition of some interesting textural variations. The purple lavender lends a dramatic touch of colour as well as texture, and fluffy* Alchemilla mollis *gives the design a new dimension.*

FLOWER ARRANGING

The beauty of flowers has inspired man for generations. In recent years, the importance of flowers in our lives has become an accepted fact and the art of flower arranging has a new status. The varied selection of arrangements shown here demonstrates the designs which are in most popular demand.

It is only possible to achieve perfect results in arranging and sending out flower designs when the groundwork has been laid with much work and skill. The arts of growing, cutting and grading, packaging and dispatching, have all been modernized in recent years, but the ability to perceive the shapes, colours and textures of nature is as important as ever.

The skill of the florist is to combine an understanding of conditioning and caring for the plant material with an artist's flair for display, as well as to have the ability to discuss and then interpret what the customer wants, based on a knowledge of the colours and qualities of the flowers available.

CONTAINERS

With so many containers and vases to choose from, it is hard to avoid being carried away when restocking in a florist's shop. From plastic to finest china – the range is simply enormous. Containers can be practical, pretty, or both; the difficulty is choosing a versatile range which will appeal to customers and enhance the flowers.

One rule of thumb is to avoid matching a 'showy' container with a busy flower arrangement. A container with clear lines and unfussy patterns can make lovely flowers look even more special, so over-decorative containers will tend to sit on the shelves for a long time.

Containers can match, contrast or harmonize with flowers and foliage, or with the furnishings and decor, but one thing they must do – unless they are to be used for dried or fabric flowers – is to hold water. Baskets, unglazed pottery and terracotta require either plastic liners or inexpensive plastic bowls that can be placed inside them.

Baskets

These are useful for informal country-style designs and for arrangements that are going to be held, perhaps by a bridesmaid or a visiting dignitary. They come in rustic styles, varnished, stained, bleached or painted. Many of the rustic styles have moss, lavender or vines twined in and out of the basketry for decorative effect. Some of the newer baskets have raised floral patterns attached to them, as in the picture.

Ceramic and glass containers

China and ceramic containers can be much more sophisticated than baskets, but there are also informal types, including jugs and cache-pots, or flower pot holders, which are suitable for uncomplicated designs with strong, bold lines.

Containers that are not fully glazed will need to be lined to make them waterproof. Make sure, also, that customers are advised to put mats beneath ceramic containers, as condensation can form underneath, and perhaps mark a polished table or sideboard.

The range of ceramic containers includes some expensive porcelain vases, and extra care should be taken when handling these. At the other end of the range, the warm glowing colours of terracotta can enhance all types of flowers, from bunches of marguerites to the most sophisticated lilies. There are dozens of terracotta designs and dozens of different glazes and finishes. The classic terracotta or clay pots need to be made waterproof before use, but they are popular with customers.

Glass containers are currently in demand, particularly for tied designs, in which the stems can look attractive. Alternatively, shells, pebbles or coloured sands can be used for decorative effect. If the flowers are to be a gift, a glass container can turn an inexpensive design into something very special. In general, glass containers have to be handled carefully, though many of those made from recycled glass are sufficiently thick to be quite durable and long lasting.

One point to bear in mind is that flower foods will not be as effective in lead crystal containers that have a high lead content.

Plastic

People are often fooled by plastic containers, picking up what they imagine to be a heavy ceramic pot, only to find they are holding a light-weight plastic, for these days the latter can have all the advantages of plastic with the good looks of china. Plastic containers of this type are not inexpensive, but they are likely to last much longer than their more breakable counterparts, and they come in a rainbow range of colours, and in many shapes, sizes and designs.

Metals

Copper cache-pots and brass containers, from goblets to coal buckets, make lovely containers for flowers. The differing textures of the flowers and the shiny containers contrast and act as a foil for each other.

Most pedestal stands designed for use in churches, hotels or marquees are made from wrought iron, and containers of this type are both adaptable and functional.

Whatever your needs, there is a wealth of containers to enhance the beauty of the flower and foliage materials.

To complement the overall effect, the container should be selected with care. The flowers and foliage can either contrast or harmonize with the container, which should be chosen to suit the décor or the occasion.

A LINE ARRANGEMENT

A sense of rhythm is essential to all types of arrangement. A curved line has a rhythm, and takes the eye through the design. Here, the repetition of the gerbera flowers leads the eye through the design, and this rhythm and movement is reinforced by loops of bear grass. The whole design is given a visual weight and strength with the use of the *Gaultheria shallon* foliage at the base of the arrangement.

A line arrangement is the basis of many other designs, the line or focal area forming the nucleus around which traditional and freestyle designs are formed.

Suitable flowers

A line arrangement demands bold single flowers, such as gerberas, carnations, roses or chrysanthemum blooms. These are then balanced by large bold leaves, and the effect is completed with fine material, such as twigs, reeds, or bear grass.

Placement

This type of design is ideal for a buffet table, where the flowers are held above the food, and it can look attractive on a reception desk. Line arrangements also work ideally when paired on either side of an altar.

WHAT YOU WILL NEED

Six gerberas, bear grass, *Gaultheria shallon*, fatshedera leaves, pottery container, plastic saucer and a cylinder of wet foam.

The bold display of gerberas is effectively complemented by the glossy black pot.

SYMMETRICAL ARRANGEMENT

T he symmetrical arrangement is a highly versatile design that is made in all sizes and for a wide variety of occasions. Part of its almost universal popularity is due to its very elegant appearance, which gives it tremendous appeal.

Prepare the container and start the design with the long foliage stems; here, cotoneaster. This will provide the outline for the design, and give protection to the flowers. The minimum height of the design is one and a half times the height (or width if it is long rather than tall) of the container. Often, the foliage is longer than the minimum, as this adds to the elegance of the design.

Proportions

The width of the design is classically two-thirds of the height, and the depth at the front of the container is a third of the height. It must be remembered that these calculations are approximate, and the size of a design will ultimately be determined by the requirements of the customer, or the position that the design will fill.

WHAT YOU WILL NEED

A container, foam, roses, lilies, two colours of spray carnations, wax flower and a selection of grey foliage types.

Secondary and focal flowers

The secondary and the focal flowers can be inserted next. The carnation sprays are added to the design so that when it is completed they will flow across the design. The focal roses move through the centre of the design in a gently curving line. The spacing between the roses is larger at the outer edges, and much smaller at the centre, which is the focal area.

To emphasize the focal area, lilies have been recessed underneath the roses. These help the visual weight and balance of the design. The crimson carnation spray strengthens the line or grouping of the lilies and adds colour contrast. The combination of the wax flower and silvery foliage; gives an airy effect to the arrangement.

Use short flowers and foliage types to complete the design and hide any small gaps. Mist the arrangement and keep cool.

1 *The foliage outline is triangular. Choose the foliage with care, to complement the container and the flowers.*

2 *The spray carnations and silver grey foliage are used to strengthen the outline; the roses flow through the centre.*

This lovely design of roses, lilies and spray carnations would make an enchanting birthday gift.

ASYMMETRICAL ARRANGEMENT

This arrangement lacks the restriction of perfect symmetry. Asymmetrical balance occurs when unequal visual weight is placed at each side of an imaginary centre line. This design has a simple but strong 'L' shape and a visual movement which usually, but not necessarily, moves from left to right.

It is important to remember that to achieve asymmetrical balance, the distribution of flowers and foliage is unequal, with longer, lighter materials, such as bud flowers, fine foliage and lighter colours horizontally placed to one side of the high vertical line, and counter-balanced on the other side with short, bold materials in darker colours.

Uses

This style of design has limited use as a commercial arrangement, for it is awkward to deliver and, unless placed at the end of the recipient's sideboard, chest or table, looks visually unbalanced. The ideal positions for an asymmetrical arrangement are either in the corner of a church window, where a design can be positioned, facing the congregation, or in matching pairs, perhaps at each end of a buffet table or placed on a mantelpiece.

Method

Choose an oblong or rectangular container. Do not place the foam in the centre of the container, but position it to one side, approximately one third of the way in from the rim of the container.

Collect the flowers and foliage. Make a strong L-shaped outline, incorporating the proportions given below. Strengthen the outline with spike flowers. Add the focal flowers in the centre, following the L-shaped outline. At the shorter side, insert short-stemmed, darker flowers, placing them horizontally. Now fill in with smaller flowers, on various levels; remember not to lose the strong outline. Lightly fill in the back of the arrangement with odd pieces of foliage, and spray it lightly with water.

WHAT YOU WILL NEED

Oblong container, one third of a foam brick, pot tape, five carnations, five stems of *Gladiolus* 'Nanus', two stems of spray chrysanthemum – one each of single and spider chrysanthemum, and five good pieces of beech.

1 *Make the outline: the height placement, one and a half times the width of the container; longest width placement, two thirds of the height, and shortest width and depth, one third.*

2 *Strengthen the L-shaped outline, using spike flowers such as* Gladiolus *'Nanus'. Add flowers for height, and the longest width and depth placements, inserting stems firmly.*

3 *Add focal flowers: five carnations are evenly spaced on various levels in the centre, forming a curving line and strengthening the visual movement of the asymmetrical flow.*

Finally, lines of darker flowers are placed on the short side, and the asymmetrical shape is carefully filled in with smaller flowers.

FOR THE SPEAKER'S TABLE

This impressive arrangement is designed for a guest speaker's table at a business, civic or social function, when it can be used to hide notes, or conceal microphones. The arrangement may also be positioned on a top table at other occasions, such as a luncheon, banquet, or wedding reception. The design should draw the eye to the top table.

Initially, this may appear to be a faced design, but in fact it must look attractive from all angles and the materials should be placed on different levels. Position the design at the centre of the table, close to the front edge. Flowers and foliage should then trail over the edge. The speaker and other VIPs should be able to see over the arrangement, however, and it must not hide them from their audience.

WHAT YOU WILL NEED

Flat oblong plastic container, wet foam, pot tape, foliage, including eucalyptus, bear grass, soft ruscus and hedera, and a range of flowers, including bold forms – lilies, gerberas, carnations, and roses, and smaller flowers, such as freesias, spray chrysanthemums and carnations, tulips and alstroemerias.

Planning

Always ask the customer for the dimensions of the table. This will dictate the size of the completed design. Remember, if the arrangement is being placed in a large hall, to select a vibrant combination of colours, bearing in mind the colours of the surrounding decor, and use bold flowers that will be clearly visible when viewed from a distance.

Construction

Prepare the container and start by making the outline, inserting the stems of the foliage firmly into the foam, and establishing the height and width of the arrangement. Ensure that trailing foliage flows over the rim of the container, and add foliage to the back of the arrangement - this is another important area.

Next, insert the bold central flowers in a graded line, with buds on the outside, and at a range of levels. Continue by strengthening the outline shape and filling in the design with smaller flowers. These should appear to radiate from the main focal flower.

Finally, recess some single flowers and leaves to give visual depth and hide the foam. Spray the arrangement with water and store it in a cool room, ready for delivery. For easy handling and delivery, pack it in a shallow box.

1 *Secure wet foam into a flat oblong container. Establish the height and width with foliage – use bear grass, hedera, soft ruscus or eucalyptus to trail over the rim of the container.*

2 *To create a visually strong focal point area, bold flowers, such as lilies, are positioned on several levels at the centre, top and back of the arrangement.*

3 *Strengthen the outline shape and fill in the design by adding smaller flowers, such as freesias, alstroemerias and tulips in diagonal lines across the arrangement.*

The completed design looks attractive from any angle and can now be placed on a speaker's table.

REGULAR CONTRACT DESIGNS

A contract design can be a ready-made display of fresh flowers and foliage, made to a set price and delivered on a certain day (usually a Monday), or displays of dried and fabric flowers and foliage which are changed at regular intervals.

Contract displays are used to decorate in numerous venues, including the following:

• Various types of shops, such as antique, jewellery, furniture or fashion shops, or large department stores;
• Hairdressers, beauty salons and health clubs;
• Offices, banks, hotels, theatres, restaurants and private homes.

Points to remember

Always use fresh, well-conditioned, first-rate flowers and foliage, with long lasting qualities. At times, this may be restrictive, but this type of material must be used to give maximum value, with the minimum of attention.

Use containers which are stable, solid, watertight, and capable of holding a good reservoir of water. Select the container to blend in with the surroundings.

All mechanics must be securely attached to the container. Plastic foam, if used, must be well soaked, but not over-saturated. All foliage and flower stems must be firmly inserted. Handtieds should be well made and firmly tied. Accessories, if used, must be appropriate and securely attached.

Suitable flowers and foliage types

Flowers with the qualities required for this type of design include alstroemerias, anthuriums, antirrhinums, carnation standards and sprays, chrysanthemum blooms and sprays, freesias, gerberas, lilies and orchids. Foliage types include beech, eucalyptus, gaultheria, nephrolepis, pittosporum and ruscus.

Position of display

The aim is for the floral display to become the centre of interest and form a talking point. To this end, position it in a prominent area, where it will easily be seen – opposite an entrance or on a reception desk, for example, or in a waiting area. Remember, however, that you must not interfere with the movement of people. Take measurements of the available space and note details of the surroundings, so that your display is suited to the venue. Traditional banks or offices demand conventional styles of display in urns, bowls and baskets. Futuristic offices and shops are complemented by freestyle designs of prestigious or exotic materials, in bold containers.

Basket
The large basket holds a quantity of well-conditioned flowers and foliage types, arranged in the traditional style. This type of design is suitable for a hotel lounge.

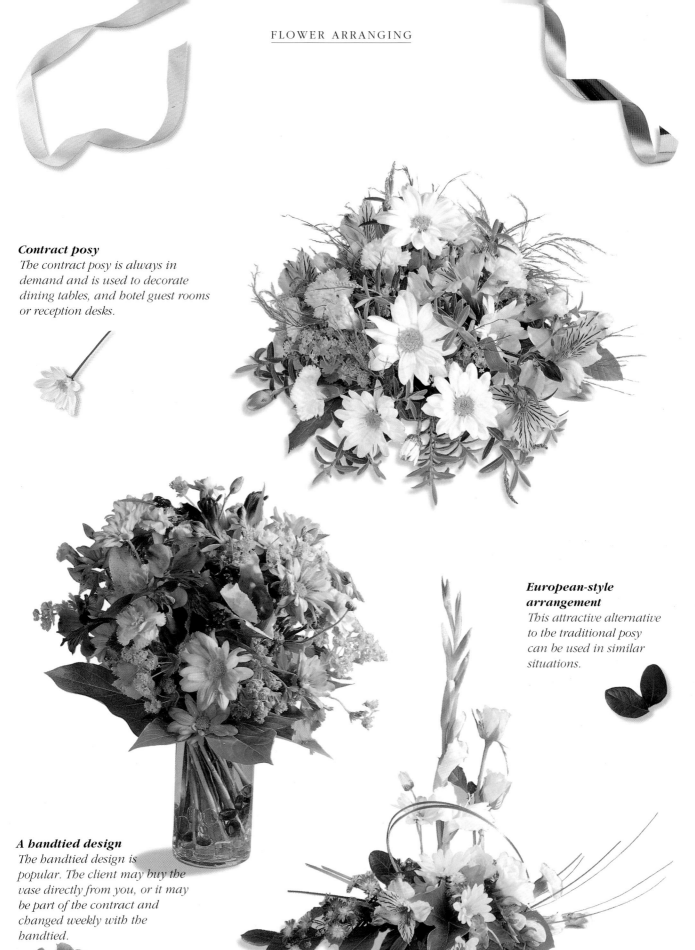

Contract posy
The contract posy is always in demand and is used to decorate dining tables, and hotel guest rooms or reception desks.

European-style arrangement
This attractive alternative to the traditional posy can be used in similar situations.

A handtied design
The handtied design is popular. The client may buy the vase directly from you, or it may be part of the contract and changed weekly with the handtied.

DESIGN FOR A TABLE

A design for a table needs to look attractive from all sides, and the flowers must be in perfect condition, as they will be viewed closely by the seated guests. The arrangement should not impede visibility or conversation across the table.

The size and proportion of the design is dictated by the size of the table and the number of place settings. Scale the flowers to the surroundings, preferably keeping them small and dainty, and coordinate the colours of the blooms with the china and table linen, and with the decor of the room or the occasion. Round and smaller tables will have a circular arrangement; a long table demands a diamond shape.

The container is either hidden completely, or can be an integral part of the setting. Always avoid highly perfumed, musky flowers, as the scent can interfere with the taste of the food.

WHAT YOU WILL NEED

A round pottery container, foam, tape, a selection of foliage types, roses, freesias, carnation spray, chrysanthemum spray, two candles to tone with the flowers, and plastic candle holders.

2 The roses and chrysanthemum spray are introduced; the roses are not taken very high, allowing the candles to provide the height.

1 The mechanics have been prepared and secured, and lines and groupings of Alchemilla mollis, Cotinus coggryia, *lonicera and hedera are taken through the design.*

3 Before too many materials are added, the candles are firmly placed in the plastic holders, which have been inserted into the foam when the mechanics were prepared.

*This design looks good
enough to eat, from all sides
– Bon appétit!*

AN ALL-ROUND ARRANGEMENT

An all-round arrangement, as the name suggests, is one that can be viewed from any side. It is sometimes more difficult to construct an all-round arrangement than a front facing type, but the end result is a useful design for the centre of a table, or even of a room.

This type of arrangement would be suitable for placement at the centre of a coffee or buffet table. On a coffee table, it would normally be made in a low dish, and on a buffet table you might use either a tall pot or a figurine. It could also be made as a very large design to stand in a foyer or reception area, on a pedestal stand or jardiniére.

WHAT YOU WILL NEED

Half a brick of wet foam, astilbe, seven red roses, two bunches of freesias, three stems of alstroemeria and five of red spray carnations, and a metal bucket.

Suitable flowers

To achieve the type of shape necessary for this design, a spike-shaped flower or foliage is ideal. The astilbe flower and foliage has been used well in the picture to form the outline shape. Other suitable flowers would be aconitums, campanulas, wax flowers, crocosmias, small or large gladioli or delphiniums, combined with ruscus, leatherleaf or eucalyptus foliage.

Once an outline has been established, a main line of more dominant flowers is taken through the centre of the design. Flowers suitable for this would include roses, carnations, gerberas, lilies and chrysanthemum blooms. The design is then completed using filler flowers, such as freesias, alstroemerias, and spray carnations, using the design principles outlined in the previous chapter to give the arrangement a pleasing shape. These include balance, harmony, scale, proportion and texture.

1 *The round container is filled with wet foam which has been well soaked. It is firmly taped into position before an outline of astilbe is formed. This is a good starting shape.*

2 *The foam has been left to protrude 3.5 – 5cm (1½ –2in) above the container, so that the flowers can flow over the edge. The outline is then strengthened with freesias and spray carnations.*

The completed arrangement looks attractive when viewed from any angle.

HOSPITAL FLOWERS

Everyone loves flowers, and someone who is ill and in hospital will appreciate them even more than usual. Flowers convey love and affection, sunshine and happiness, making the patient feel cherished, and it is very important that a florist should select appropriate flowers to send in such cases.

This beautiful handtied display of long-lasting flowers, including lilies, carnations and spray carnations, is arranged ready to be placed into a vase.

Flowers for hospitals

Hospitals are normally very warm, especially the maternity wards, and it is therefore essential that any flowers sent are long-lasting species, which can tolerate heat. Spring flowers and roses, unfortunately, do not last long in warm temperatures, but there are some suitable flowers and foliages for consideration, including the following:

    carnations and spray carnations
    Alstroemeria hybrids
    Astrantia major
    wax flowers
    chrysanthemum blooms and sprays
    Cymbidium orchids
    lilies
    Limonium sinuatum
    Triteleia hybrids
    Ruscus hypophyllum

    Aster ericoides
    Eucalyptus hybrids
    leatherleaf

All flowers should be well conditioned before being sent out. Make sure the stems have been cut correctly and that they have stood in water for at least three to four hours, but preferably overnight, to get a good drink before being used.

Suitable containers

Containers sent out to hospitals should be flat bottomed and able to stand firmly. The flowers are normally placed either on the bedside locker or on a table in the centre of the ward. If they are to go on the locker, a small arrangement in a saucer is the most appropriate, as there is normally very little space. Pedestal-style containers are usually avoided, as they are inclined to be top heavy and are easily knocked over.

Something a little different – the exquisite African violet has been planted in a purple basket to enhance the colour, and a variegated ivy has been added to complete the arrangement. The basket is lined with black plastic to stop water leakages.

Designs suitable for hospitals

Hospital staff are very busy people, and by sending gift-wrapped flowers in cellophane you will increase their workload, as they will have to arrange the flowers. It is far more practical to send a handtied bunch, which only needs to be placed in a vase of water.

If an arrangement is to be sent, it is sensible to use a container large enough to hold a good quantity of water, so that staff are not having to top it up all the time. In any case, flowers transpire more and therefore use up far more water when in warm conditions than they do when the surroundings are cool.

Delivery to hospital

It is very important when taking orders for delivery to hospitals that all details are accurately recorded.

Mrs E. Jones, Countess of Chester Hospital, will NOT do; the full name and address must be given:

Mrs Elizabeth Jones,
Ward 4,
Countess of Chester Hospital,
Liverpool Road,
Chester.

It is also necessary to make sure you have the customer's telephone number in case there are any problems. The patient may have been discharged and returned home to an area outside the shop's delivery range.

To ensure that you have all this information to hand is a very important part of the florist's training – just as important, in fact, as being able to make a carnation buttonhole or a handtied bunch of flowers. A certain amount of practical training of this type will take place in college, but it is also essential for senior staff in the workplace to make sure that junior members of staff recognize the importance of such practicalities. Individual shops will have their own particular procedures, and training must be an ongoing and continuous process.

Colour

When choosing flowers, customers often ask for the recipient's favourite colour, but if they do not know this they may ask the florist for advice. If the flowers are to celebrate the birth of a boy or girl, this is easy, as it is normal to send pink for a girl and

A delightful arrangement, firmly set into a flat-bottomed bowl, this design would sit securely on a bedside locker or table. The charming pink lilies form a strong focal area.

either blue or yellow for a boy. Blue flowers are sometimes difficult to acquire, and blue ribbon is used as a substitute. Yellow and orange flowers always look bright and cheerful, while red makes the room look warm. White, cream and blue flowers are restful, and a good choice for someone who is very ill. It is also helpful to find out for whom the flowers are being bought; men seem to prefer bright strong colours, such as reds, burgundy and rusts, whereas older ladies like mauves, lilacs and pastel colours. Children seem to prefer bright colours.

NEW BABY ARRANGEMENT

The arrival of a new baby is a special occasion that needs a carefully thought out design.

The choice of flowers and foliage is important, with colour being the main design principle. The traditional pastel colours are most appropriate, with soft pinks and white being associated with girls and pale blues and white for boys.

It also makes a nice touch to incorporate a small gift in the arrangement, such as a rattle or pair of booties.

WHAT YOU WILL NEED

Roses, carnation sprays, chrysanthemum sprays, hydrangeas, leather leaf and sprigs of heather.

2 *Build up the outline of the design. Place roses in the centre to give height and arrange smaller cut materials on the outer edges. Recess short flowers and foliage in the foam to create depth.*

1 *Line the basket then fill it with foam and moss. Attach the booties to long strips of satin ribbon.*

3 *Fill in the arrangement with carnation sprays, chrysanthemums and roses. Add sprigs of heather for texture and contrast. The foam should now be completely hidden.*

A lovely gift for a mum and new baby, the booties can be worn or kept as a memento.

EUROPEAN ARRANGEMENTS

European or continental arrangements are, as the name implies, a style of design that originated in Europe and is totally different from the standard British arrangement. A European design is far more structured, balanced but not symmetrical, its impact coming from groupings of bold materials. Every leaf and flower shows, and must therefore be perfectly groomed. The design shown here is based on the parallel concept, but here materials are also brought out horizontally as well as vertically. It is important with this type of design to use bold materials and a variety of shapes and textures in order to give the arrangement its impact.

The foam is covered with mosses and fungi and also by recessing some low lying flowers.

This type of arrangement, with its clean lines, looks very good in modern buildings, and because it contains very few flowers in a reasonably large piece of foam, it can be kept well watered and is long lasting.

WHAT YOU WILL NEED

Pink and white hyacinths, double tulips, gerberas, 'Jacaranda' roses, cornus, *Helleborus orientalis, Arum italicum*, pink decorative wire, wet foam and a plastic container.

1 *Wet foam is cut and fitted into the container, leaving approximately 12mm (½in) rising above the top of the container.*

2 *Fungi and moss are used to conceal the foam, cornus gives height to the design, and flowers and foliage in a range of forms and textures provide the interest.*

Materials chosen for a
European design must be
perfect and dramatic, for
maximum impact.

A LARGE TABLE ARRANGEMENT

This is an impressive table design, although it uses only a small amount of flower materials. It is a large arrangement, and while it is not the diamond shape traditionally used for a long table, it would be an acceptable design for a large table, perhaps seating ten or twelve people.

The amount of detail in this design is appropriate for the close attention that table arrangements receive from those seated. The flowers and foliage have light and delicate fragrances that will not interfere with the taste of the food being served.

The foliage

There is a minimal quantity of flower materials, but an arrangement of this type does require a substantial range of interesting foliage types. A good textural contrast is provided in this design, the larger and shinier leaves of the *Hedera helix* 'Buttercup' acting as a foil to the *Cassinia fulvida* (at the front

of the design), and to other dainty-leaved and matt-textured varieties of foliage. The creams and greens are offset by the dark alder cones and the deep bronze of the beech leaves.

The foliage has been placed around the ring in groups of three. One grouping is positioned on the outer edge, with the next on the top of the frame, and the last grouping is inserted in the inner part of the ring. This is repeated with the other foliage types. In this way, a rhythmic pattern emerges.

The flowers

There are five main groupings of flowers, each featuring a different flower, and distinct in size and form while harmonizing in colour. The flowers are used on short stems, so the more expensive long-stemmed materials need not be used.

Candles

Usually, it is preferable to start with the candles, but in this design the candles were inserted last. If, for handling reasons, you intend to work this way round, always mark where the candles are to be inserted.

Candles always impart a mellow, romantic quality to flowers, and the soft cream candles give a pleasing light to this design.

WHAT YOU WILL NEED

A 30cm (12in) foam ring, roses, lilies, carnation spray, chrysanthemum spray, freesias, a selection of foliage types, alder cones, and three 25cm (10in) church candles.

1 *The foliage is placed in a circular outline around the frame. Conifer, ivy, moss, Jerusalem sage, alchemilla and other foliage types are inserted around the frame in groups, giving pattern to the design.*

2 *Other kinds of foliage and the alder cones have been added, the dark beech leaves contrasting with the lime greens of the other materials. The five flower groupings are almost complete, and only the roses and a few more flowers remain to be added.*

An enchanting centrepiece, this would be a pleasure to view while eating good food.

A HANDTIED POSY

Handtied bunches are a delightful way of giving flowers. The stems are clear of leaves and the flowers are arranged. All the recipient has to do is to re-cut the stem ends and place the flowers in a vase of water. Handtied bunches have always been part of the European florist's repertoire; nearly every assistant in a florist's shop will arrange flowers in the hand as they are bought, the stems having already been stripped of their leaves before they were placed on display.

Spiralling

Starting with one good strong stem, the other materials are added as the bunch is turned in the hand. This distributes the flowers evenly around the main stem, and forms a good all-round shape. The top of the design may be flat or domed, depending on the personal preference of the florist making the design. There is no correct method – just different styles, chosen as appropriate.

Tying off

One way of tying off is to wrap a plastic tie around the stems several times, and then thread it through the stems to secure it. The other options are to tie the design firmly with twine, knotting it securely, or to wrap pot tape around the stems to hold them firmly in place.

Gift wrapping

Once tied, the bunch can be gift wrapped with cellophane in many different ways. The wrapping is used more for attraction than to protect the flowers. A ribbon bow completes the design. It is worth adding a care card to the display, as many customers still imagine that they have to undo the bunch and rearrange the flowers.

After stripping all the stems and arranging the flowers into individual groups, they are then arranged in the hand, with the stems spiralling. The bunch is tied together with twine or pot tape.

The dainty handtied posy, if tied with a satin ribbon, could be carried by a bride or bridesmaid.

CAKE AND TABLE DECORATIONS

Delicate fresh flower and foliage, with pretty ribbons, daintily arranged, make a charming cake-top decoration for various occasions, including anniversaries and engagements and, of course, weddings.

The wedding cake is an important feature of the reception, but if placed in front of the bride and groom it can hide them from their guests. Suggest that the cake has a place of honour on a separate table, to be decorated by you. This will create interest and provide a centrepiece for the cutting of the cake.

Always ask the bride for details of the cake, as today's cakes are very individual, and there are innumerable styles and sizes. Some cakes may take the form of initials or hearts, but traditional cakes are either round or square, with one, two, three or more

---

WHAT YOU WILL NEED

Three good stems of pale pink spray roses, two to three stems of Singapore orchids, a stem of lilac, one bunch of freesia, stems of *Asparagus plumosus*, *Alchemilla mollis*, ruscus and *Bupleurum griffithii*, and a foam bump.

---

tiers, supported on pillars. The current trend is for perspex or steel stands, which suspend the cakes on various levels.

The traditional container was a silver vase, though sometimes a wine glass was used instead, but hiding the foam used to be a problem. Now the foam can simply be surrounded with crumpled strips of cellophane which, when filled with flowers, looks like crushed ice. Specially-designed foam bump on a plastic base provides an excellent foundation, making assembly quick and easy.

Method

Work on a sheet of paper. First prepare any ribbon bows that are required. Lightly soak the foam. The construction is similar to that of a small and dainty open posy: first make the circular shape using lightweight foliage and flower buds; firmly insert a rose bud, placing it vertically in the centre of the foam; create a domed shape using the other materials, and fill in with dainty flowers and foliage on various levels, while creating an elevated profile. Finally, recess the lilac, lightly spray and store until required.

1 *Lightly soak the foam. Make a circular outline, using fine foliage, bud flowers, and ribbon streamers at regular intervals.*

2 *Create a dome by inserting a central rose bud. Add other buds, making an elevated profile.*

Position the main cake
decoration on the top
tier. Add another dainty
flowing design on the
second tier. To bring the
effect together, position a
large cascading
arrangement on the
front of the table.

PEW ENDS

Everyone loves pew ends. They guide the bride down the aisle to the altar; they make the scene complete, and they help to give the church a fairytale appearance. In addition, pew ends are expected to be a low-cost item, and they can be a good way of using up short flowers.

Traditional style
If the wedding is in a traditional church or cathedral, the flowers are generally massed, with little space left between them and with lots of foliage. The typical arrangements to choose for the occasion would be large triangle-shaped pedestals, and the pew ends would be in keeping with these. Again, they would be triangular in shape, but in this case with the length running down the design, and with flowers and foliage massed together.

Modern style
In a modern building, it is far more appropriate to make the arrangements modern. Use bold flowers and leaves, and lots of space. Here again, the pew ends would echo the larger arrangements.

WHAT YOU WILL NEED

Foam holder, hedera foliage, *Alchemilla mollis*, two stems of white single chrysanthemum spray, and a length of ribbon.

1 *Foam holder is soaked for three to four minutes in water, before an outline of hedera is pushed firmly into the wet foam.*

2 *A large bow of poly-tie ribbon is held firmly in place by a 0.90mm (20 gauge) wire. A single white chrysanthemum spray completes the design.*

The top pew end is in the modern style; the bottom design is traditional, and would be in keeping with an older building.

PEDESTAL ARRANGEMENT

This design never fails to impress and stimulate interest, simply because of its size and the amounts of flowers and foliage used. To achieve the full impact, it is necessary to position the pedestal in a spacious area, or the perspective becomes unbalanced. Suitable settings include churches, marquees, and foyers in large offices, banks, hotels and theatres. Whatever the situation, remember to keep the proportions, style and colour combinations of the arrangement in tune with the surroundings.

Basically, there are two styles of pedestal: the traditional wrought-iron stand, sprayed black, cream or white, which has a container that slots into the stand, or stands made in wood, hardboard, plastic or china, a separate bowl being placed on top.

WHAT YOU WILL NEED

A stand, a deep bowl, two bricks of wet foam and two pieces for wedging, wire mesh, pot tape, and a range of striking flowers and foliage types.

2 Establish the shape, strengthening the outline with foliage, and add bold leaves to the centre.

1 Fill a solid container, holding a good reservoir of water, with two bricks of wet foam, wedged in with two pieces of foam. For security, crumpled wire mesh is placed over the foam and attached with pot tape.

3 Grade the focal flowers through the centre of design, placing them on different heights. The main focal flower is placed at the front of the foam, at the base of the first placement. The profile is now established.

The foliage outline and focal flowers are now linked with lines of small flowers. Bold and trailing foliage types complete the design.

DRIED AND FABRIC FLOWERS

At one time, dried flowers were generally considered drab and colourless; now, this has changed dramatically, and the floristry industry is supplied by specialist growers who produce an amazing range of dried flowers and foliage types, together with seed heads of every description. In addition to species grown at home, unusual materials, imported from exotic locations, are available at wholesalers.

Materials are now dried and coloured to every tint, tone and shade on the colour wheel, and as the range of dried materials has developed, so too has that of fabric flowers and foliage. Now available with natural colourings and botanically correct detailing, they can be so realistic that many customers at first believe them to be fresh. Complementing this development is an attractive new range of baskets and containers, as well as delightful ribbons.

WALL SWAGS

Wall swags may be used for many occasions or seasons; blue pine, cones and red ribbon can make a wonderful Christmas design, for example, while herbs and garlic can be combined in a culinary swag that would brighten any kitchen.

Bases
Designs may be made on a variety of bases. These include pieces of wood with dry foam either taped or glued in place, foam frames such as wreaths or open hearts, or purpose-made bases such as Raquettes.

Materials
A wall swag is normally designed as a permanent feature in a room, and either fabric or dried flowers are therefore ideal. Fabric flowers are now available in a wonderful array of colours and shapes. Being on wire stems, they are easily secured into dry foam, though a glue gun may be used for extra security. Most types of flower normally used in arrangements are also available in dried form and, here again, the hard stems are easily pushed firmly into the foam.

2 *Hairpins secure lichen moss to the plastic-coated surface. The outline is then formed from fabric hollyhocks and peonies, with dried artichoke heads.*

WHAT YOU WILL NEED

A selection of dried and fabric flowers, lichen moss, fabric, hairpins, 0.71mm (22 gauge) green annealed wires, and an Oasis Raquette.

1 *A heavy hanging wire has been attached to an Oasis Raquette. Rich tapestry fabric is secured with 0.71mm (22 gauge) green annealed wires.*

3 *Plant materials must be added to the sides as well as the front of the arrangement. Large leaves add variety to the shapes and textures.*

The vibrant colours and exciting shapes of this wall swag make it a dramatic design that would enhance any room.

TOPIARY TREES

As with other garden ideas, florists have adapted the art of clipping shrubs to make the very appealing and popular designs we see today. Small trees will sit comfortably on a coffee table, looking attractive from all sides. Large designs have a distinctive poise, and look striking in hotels, churches or marquees. The range of designs shown here and on the following pages was made with fabric and dried materials.

Preparation

The top-heavy weight distribution makes it advisable to have a substantial base to ensure that a topiary design is well balanced when completed. Here, the pole is fixed into a dry-hard, fast-setting clay that is very heavy, providing the finished arrangement with a stable base.

About 5cm (2in) of the dry plastic foam is 'cored' from the sphere, making it easier to push onto the ribboned pole. The lilac paper ribbon, covering the globe, is pinned into place. Texture is important when using fabric flowers, and dried materials add contrast to the composition. A further addition is the same paper ribbon, which is also scrunched and then glued in place.

Knife slits in the ribbon covering the globe make it simple to insert small blossoms into the dried foam. Placing the flowers in lines around the circumference to keep a good shape, the larger flowers are evenly spaced over the topiary tree. The small poppy seed heads and other dried flowers are scattered between the large blossoms, but in groups rather than singly.

Design unity

In general, topiary trees are filled in with flowers and other materials, to hide the mechanics, but here the ribbon covering the sphere is a feature of the composition. The scrunched ribbon on the globe is conveyed through the design by gluing it to the trunk of the tree and then down onto the container. The design becomes an integral whole, each part being joined with another.

Sprigs of blossom at the base of the trunk give a final flourish to the arrangement.

WHAT YOU WILL NEED

Selection of round or mass dried flower forms, seed heads, fabric flowers, lilac paper ribbon, ribboned pole, glue and glue gun, pins, dry foam sphere, ceramic pot and fast-setting clay.

1 *The flowers selected are round or mass forms reflecting the shape of this topiary tree.*

2 *A ribboned pole is pushed firmly into the clay and the sphere is covered in paper ribbon. Hot glue on top of the pole helps to secure the sphere.*

3 *Insert materials into the foam. Start by placing the blooms around the sphere in quarter segments. Small flowers are glued in place.*

Finishing touches include the fabric blossoms at the base of the design and the scrunched ribbon around the container.

TOPIARY DESIGNS

Topiary designs have developed greatly, and many variations on the original theme can be produced. The current fashion trend is to use an old terracotta flower pot as a container, with a single support stem of natural wood, such as birch, the sphere being covered with either lichen or bun moss. This represents the 'natural rustic' look, developed by many florists as their designer style.

Topiary trees are very versatile, ranging in size from miniature designs to imposing trees some 3.75m (12ft) in height, used to decorate churches, hotels or marquees for various celebrations and events.

Materials

In the original garden topiary, fresh box was sculptured into geometric shapes and life-like animal forms. These days, the florist has an endless supply of fresh and dried materials from which to choose. Styles can be very imaginative, with one, two or three placements. Forms vary from cones and spheres to free-style groups. Natural support stems range from a single piece of wood, such as birch, to several pieces of wood grouped together, or stems of willow used in a twisted effect. For an impressive tree, a large multi-stemmed branch will provide an interesting structure and give imposing height.

Above *Split cinnamon sticks are glued to a support stem. The dry foam cone is covered by narrow curving lines of nuts, leaves and lichen moss, over-wrapped with copper wire.*

Right *Two-tier topiary was created with graded spheres of dry foam. The grouped combinations of materials include shells, lichen moss, roses, hydrangea heads, seed heads, fabric leaves, and rosettes of shot satin ribbon. The ceramic container and saucer are an integral part of the design.*

Special designs

Sculptured trees of dried and preserved materials can be individually designed for specialist clothes, furniture, shoe/handbag, kitchen utensil and food shops (to name but a few), as well as for offices, leisure centres and beauty or hairdressing salons.

Such designs might be suggested as an alternative contract arrangement. Hotel corridors and bedrooms are perfect settings for topiary trees, as are private homes.

Above Two groups of fabric sunflowers, statice, leaves and coloured wheat decorate a multi-stemmed branch; a third group at the base completes the design. Bun moss covers the spheres and the top of the glazed pot.

Top left A sprayed bronze container holds a highly textured tree with bands of gilded and copper-sprayed cones and foliage, interlaced with foil ribbon.

Left A classical urn holds a large dry foam sphere, covered with dyed green lichen moss. Small dried loaves, apple slices, leaves and raffia bows are grouped together. The tree is then placed on a marble base.

BASKETS

Baskets are an ideal accompaniment for flowers. They are available in a multitude of materials and an amazing assortment of shapes and sizes, so it is possible to purchase a suitable basket for any occasion.

Small delicate baskets can be used for designs to be carried, large ones for planted displays, and all the sizes in between for fresh, fabric or dried arrangements.

With a coarsely-woven rustic basket, use a profusion of dried country-style flowers, such as larkspur, yarrow, alchemilla and tansy.

Fabric flowers in a small pastel-coloured basket can create a wonderfully romantic display for a bride or her attendants. Complete the design with a bow of good-quality fabric ribbon.

It is a good idea to link the colour of the basket to the arrangement, so choose pale pastel shades to fill a straw-coloured willow basket, or vibrant exotic flowers to complement baskets of woven palm or bamboo.

The natural texture and colour of the basket in the picture makes it an obvious choice to display this wonderful array of dried materials. The colours extend from pale through to dark green, and from pink to red and burgundy. The materials include poppy seed heads, amaranthus, celosia, Spanish moss, green wheat, *Anigozanthos rufus* and statice.

Texture

Texture plays an extremely important part in a dried arrangement. Leaves, flowers, seed heads and grasses all have different textures, and it is important to mix them, especially in a design of similar colours. Grouped materials also have far more impact than flowers dotted around, and the mixture of red and green in this basket is a complementary colour harmony (see page 62) that balances perfectly.

Strong groupings of both textures and colours will give the arrangement a dramatic visual appeal. The handle of the basket has been removed so as not to detract from the flowers.

This design would be ideal for use in a lounge or reception area, on a low table, where it would be viewed from above.

WHAT YOU WILL NEED

Statice and a selection of other dried materials, dry foam, glue gun, 0.71mm (22 gauge) green annealed wires, and a basket to complement the colours of the flowers.

1 *Dry foam is firmly secured into the basket using a glue gun. The materials are placed into small bunches and secured together with 0.71mm (22 gauge) green annealed wires.*

2 *The basket is lightly filled with statice, the stems firmly pushed into the foam. All the wired materials are then added, being grouped together to strengthen the form and colour, and to give the arrangement more impact.*

The completed design is ideal for a low coffee table, where the flowers will be viewed from above.

A HANDTIED BOUQUET

Creamy roses and dried flowers in soft bronzes and browns are assembled together in a simple tied bouquet. This is a design that has wide appeal, and the popularity of fresh handtied bouquets has encouraged florists to offer such bouquets in the longer-lasting dried and fabric flowers.

This type of bouquet is suitable for many occasions and situations – as a gift, it would leave a wonderful impression with the recipient; as a bouquet for a bride or bridesmaid, it has a romantic simplicity, and as a vase arrangement for a hotel or reception desk, it heralds a friendly greeting.

For each of these occasions, a slightly different emphasis would be necessary. The gift, for example, would need some special

gift wrapping; a bridal bouquet would be completed with a luxurious bow, while an attractive and carefully selected vase would complement the bouquet and surrounding decor at a reception desk.

Materials and accessories

Selecting materials and accessories that harmonize in colour and yet contrast in form and texture takes a certain amount of effort and practice, for the different components must produce a harmonious whole.

Fresh materials possess a greater volume of petals and foliage than dried ones, so to achieve a good visual effect, the dried flowers have been placed in strong groupings through the bouquet shown here.

To ensure that the arrangement is completely stable, pebbles or cleaned gravel are used to weight the bottom of the vase. Once the tying is completed, the stems can be cut to length and the bouquet can be placed in the terracotta container or wrapped, ready for presentation.

WHAT YOU WILL NEED

Fabric roses, fabric blossom sprays, dried larkspur, grasses, poppy seed heads, twine to tie the bouquet, and a terracotta vase.

1 *Tied designs are made with the spiralling method (see page 196). Not only do the stems look attractive, but the spiralling helps the materials to fan out, making good use of space around the flowers.*

2 *The shape of the bouquet is becoming clear. The strong groupings of dried materials can be seen, particularly the hare's-tail grass* (Lagurus ovatus) *and ornamental poppies* (Papaver somniferum).

Teamed with a terracotta vase, the tied bouquet evokes an autumnal abundance. Creamy roses draw the eye into the design.

A SEMI-CRESCENT BOUQUET

I n a busy shop, fabric and dried flowers have many advantages for wedding designs. In particular, if the wedding is at a peak selling time, this type of order helps to reduce pressure, as designs can be made in advance, during a quiet period.

Fabric flowers and dried materials are available in almost all colours, offering a permanent memento of the day, as well as an attractive option for the bride who is allergic to fresh materials.

Method of construction

Where possible, select materials that have natural curves. Collect all materials, tools and equipment together. Support-wire and mount materials as appropriate. Tape and form the flowers and foliage into branching units.

When you have completed stage two, below, add units of flowers and foliage on all levels, leading to the main focal point. This gives an elevated profile, and links the lines of flowers and foliage, creating visual movement. Recess some single flowers and leaves to give visual depth and hide the mechanics.

Completing the bouquet

To complete the bouquet, helping to hide the mechanics and give an attractive finish, place three or more single leaves with their reverse side against the binding point of the bouquet. Bind them in position if necessary. Trim out the wires in the handle and cover it with tape (white, if white or pastel ribbon is being used). Ensure that the binding point is hidden. Add the bow and firmly cover the handle with ribbon, tying it securely under the bow. Check, making minor adjustments as required.

Complete the order, then carefully pack it in a labelled storage box and place in dry store until required. Check and make any adjustments before delivery.

1 *Establish the semi-crescent outline with spike forms. Add graded focal flowers, the main one at the centre. Secure all wires at the binding point, remembering ⅓ – ⅔ proportions – the wires now form the handle.*

2 *Strengthen the semi-crescent outline by adding units of two, three or more small flowers. These link the outline spikes with the focal flowers. All materials must appear to radiate from the focal flower.*

The complete bouquet, with a garland headdress, is now ready for the bride – a smaller version could be carried by an adult brides-maid.

A PATCHWORK POMANDER

Historically, floral and citrus pomanders were aromatic spheres carried to ward off infections, which people used to believe were spread through bad smells. Today, pomanders made with fresh, dried or fabric flowers are a popular novelty design for the smallest of the bride's attendants, their firm construction enabling them to withstand a certain amount of handling by little hands.

The sphere can be massed with one type of flower – roses or carnation sprays are favoured – or they can have a mixture of small flowers and ribbons. The patchwork effect of this particular design is also called sculptured or textured.

The colour, flowers and fabrics for this pomander were selected to harmonize with the child's dress while complementing the bride's wedding dress. The satin ribbon con-trasts beautifully with the small dried roses, tiny fabric flowers, and dried reindeer moss, and together they make a very appealing combination.

Textural variety

Iridescent satin ribbons cover a rope handle and tails. The ribbon is wrapped rather roughly around the rope to link in with the textured massing of the base. Small units of ribbon have been introduced into the pomander to give an impression that soft rose petals have been mixed with the tiny dried flowers. Reindeer moss is pinned between the materials and ribbons, both to add to the textural range, and to fill in any small gaps, concealing the dry foam sphere. Finally, the pomander is teamed with a matching garland headdress.

1 *The handle and tails are each firmly mounted on a stub wire and inserted into the dry foam sphere. Roses, small fabric flowers and ribbons are mounted on fine stub wires.*

2 *Flowers and ribbons are added in a circular outline. The materials must be inserted closely against the base of the sphere – if they are too far away the design may look heavy and out of proportion with the handle.*

WHAT YOU WILL NEED

A sphere of dried foam, thick rope or cord, satin ribbon, reindeer moss, small dried and artificial flowers, a selection of wires, and florists' tape.

Inserting the materials

Some of the fabric flowers can be cut to length and inserted directly into the dry foam. The dried materials require double leg wire mounts (see page 51). The ribbon units should be mounted and taped for security (see page 52).

The handle of the pomander and the tails are single-leg mounted, to allow the wire to pass completely through the sphere. This method gives the handle total security, ensuring that it will not slip out of the sphere.

The ribbon units are evenly spaced over the dry foam, creating the patchwork effect. The flowers are grouped a little, particularly the small drieds, so that they will then be in better scale with the larger ribbon units.

Adding fragrance

Fragrance is added to the pomander by putting tiny drops of pot pourri oils on some of the dried roses.

If the pomander and garland have been made before the wedding date, they can be carefully stored in tissue paper to protect them from sunlight and dust.

Harmonized with a matching garland headdress, this feather-light pomander could be comfortably carried by a small bridesmaid.

SPECIAL OCCASIONS

Dried and fabric flowers come in a wealth of colours and textures, and when a long-lasting display is needed they are an ideal medium to use. Gone are the days of dusty faded arrangements; instead, vibrant but subtle colours are now achieved by freeze and kiln drying.

An immense range of dried plant materials is now available, but it is important to keep them out of damp atmospheres, and bright direct sunlight must also be avoided as displays can fade badly. Fabric flowers are also available in every colour and most varieties. These days, they are so realistic that it is almost impossible to distinguish them from the real thing.

Fabric and dried materials may either be mixed in a design or used separately. They can be displayed in a host of containers, as illustrated, including a heart frame, a foam-filled tray, a foam ring or a basket.

The stems of the fabric and dried flowers, being hard and firm, can easily be pushed into the foam, though a glue gun may be used for extra security.

Proprietary dust-repellent sprays may be used to protect and clean the materials. If looked after well, dried and fabric flowers will give pleasure and are an invaluable addition to the florist's repertoire.

A European garland arrangement

This sophisticated design is made on a dry foam ring and would be ideal for conferences and meetings.

A wedding day memento

Richly-coloured fabric flowers provide an echo of their fresh counterparts and are a reminder of a special wedding bouquet carried by the bride.

Welcome to a new home

Dried materials are glued into a heart frame which has been edged with a hessian ribbon.

A bridesmaid's basket design

Fabric flowers are arranged in dry foam which has been glued into a pale peach basket — a charming gift to place on a dressing table after the wedding.

A parallel arrangement

A striking mixture of blue and green dried and fabric materials makes an unusual present for Mother's Day.

ASKHAM BRYAN COLLEGE

YORK

133

A GARLAND OR WREATH

This type of design is becoming more popular, giving the florist the opportunity to sell a different style of decoration. This type of base can be used as the foundation for an attractive wall design, which might be positioned over a fireplace or on the wall in a hotel, restaurant, shop or private home.

Florists' wholesalers now offer a wide range of decorative bases. The rings are made in materials ranging from straw, vine, and twigs and branches of suitable trees, especially willow, to scented materials, such as lavender and other herbs. The finish may be natural, varnished or coloured, and all types of preserved, dried and artificial flowers, foliage, seed heads and fruits may be used.

The design may be a single spray or cluster, two or three of these, evenly spaced, or informal groupings of materials, covering the top of the frame.

Basic method

Collect the base, ribbons, equipment and all materials. Prepare the frame mechanics as shown below; for added security, the foam may be taped in place after it has been trimmed to shape. Pin clusters of lichen moss to hide the foundation and make an attractive finish, and then establish the outline, placing bold leaves at the centre for visual depth. Position focal point materials (here, seed heads) in a diagonal line, the largest at the centre.

Now add flowers and foliage in lines and groupings, filling the outline shape and placing flowers and leaves on different levels, to create an elevated profile.

Ribbon loops are positioned near the focal point areas, while single leaves and flowers are recessed. Finally, add streamers and glue the bow into position. For greater security, all materials can be glued in place.

WHAT YOU WILL NEED

A decorative (willow) base, selection of flowers, seed heads, branches and lichen moss, stub wires, hairpins, reel of attractive ribbon, glue gun, dry foam brick, and pot tape.

Overwrap base with ribbon and glue in place. Glue a third of a foam brick to the base and trim to shape with a sharp knife. Hairpin moss over foam, then add outline materials.

The remaining materials, including the bow and streamers, have been attached to the frame, which is now ready to be hung.

AN ARRANGEMENT

One way of producing a visually interesting display when using dried and artificial flowers is to incorporate plenty of contrasting forms and textures. The spike materials in this design provide the ideal contrast to the rounded forms of the larger leaves and flowers, while the fluffy grasses offer an excellent visual foil to the smooth surfaces of the foliage.

The principles applying to shape and the method of constructing a triangular design in dried and fabric flowers are the same as if the arrangement were being made with fresh materials. There are differences, however, when it comes to the selection of materials,

because dried and fabric flowers do not have the volume, or bulk, of fresh ones, and more materials are therefore required.

Balance

To avoid a muddled finish, it is usually best, as with the arrangement shown here, in which the centre is dominated by peonies, to add the smaller or less striking materials in groupings. Here, all the stems appear to emanate from behind the focal peony.

Most flowers and foliage can be placed directly into the dried foam. Delicate stems, such as the grasses and helichrysum in this arrangement, will need to be mounted on stub wires.

Large leaves placed towards the centre of the design give visual weight and a well balanced look to the completed arrangement. The design has a clear outline, and its profile has been built up to look attractive from the front and sides.

> **WHAT YOU WILL NEED**
>
> Peonies, dried grasses, foliage and flowers, and small fabric flowers, reindeer moss, dry foam, hairpins, selection of wires and terracotta container.

1 *Reindeer moss is pinned to the surface of the dry foam, which has been placed in a terracotta container. The outline is established with the spike materials, positioned in strong groupings.*

2 *All the focal flowers are added in a gentle line through the centre of the design. The focal point is the largest peony, facing forwards; small fabric flowers are placed as a foil to the peonies.*

A pleasing combination of fabric and dried flowers, its neutral colours would make this arrangement a desirable addition to the decor of any room.

DRYING FLOWERS

Perhaps it is a reflection on our own hectic lifestyles that we need lasting objects of natural beauty around us. The popularity of dried flowers and arrangements has remained constant for several years.

Dried materials have an ability to fit into any decor; larkspur, roses and gypsophila have a soft countryside appeal, while exotic pods and seed heads have a dramatic quality more suited to a modern decor. The dried flowers are available in a vast range of textures and forms and, with the introduction of improved dyes, many colours. Country garden pastels – pinks, creams and china blues – are being replaced in popularity by the rich tones of burgundies, forest green and velvety blues and purples.

Mixed bouquets or bunches are useful for those who wish to arrange at home, but many customers prefer to buy arrangements that have been designed to their particular requirements. The use of fabric, freeze-dried, and the new-look paper flowers broadens the range and the appeal of the designs that a florist can now offer.

Drying on the premises

Professional growers of dried flowers have temperature-controlled warehouses with dehumidifiers to speed up the drying process. In the florist's shop, the same flowers and foliage can be air dried. The process is very simple, but it takes longer. Because it is so simple, many florists underestimate the potential that air drying has for even the smallest business. Materials dried 'in house' give the arrangements created a personal touch, and are a way of selling cut materials that have not proved popular when sold fresh.

So what is the best way to air dry? An area with a good circulation of air is required, out of direct sunlight. The ceiling area of a business meets these qualifications and generally provides an ideal place for drying flowers. Lengths of twine or binding wire can be strung across the ceiling so that bunches of flowers and foliage can be attached to it, upside down. As well as having a rustic charm, viewed from below, these attractive bunches of flowers, herbs and foliage will eventually serve a practical purpose.

Drying tips

Choose materials that are dry; flowers should not be fully open, because they will open out a little as they dry. Be experimental, and try out as many flowers and foliage types as possible. Put the materials into medium-to-small bunches, as these will dry faster than large bunches. To hold bunches together, use elastic bands rather than twine, as the former will automatically tighten as the stems loose their moisture. This will prevent dry flower stems falling out of the bunches and onto the floor.

If the flowers are hung upside down, they will not droop when dried, and will keep their general shape. Drying times depend on conditions in the shop and the size of the flowers, but anything from two to four weeks is normal.

Petals and foliage from unsuccessful experiments are not entirely lost, and can be added to pot pourri mixtures.

The final stage in air drying is to treat materials with a fire retardant. Several of these are available in aerosol form. Follow the manufacturer's instructions for maximum effect.

Tropical cut flowers, such as the members of the Proteaceae family, can successfully and easily be dried. Australian honeysuckle (*Banksia*), king and queen proteas and pincushion proteas can 'double up' by being used in fresh arrangements before being dried. Foliage such as eucalyptus can be air dried and the many and varied species do keep a little of their fragrance for some time.

Kangaroo paw (*Anigozanthos* sp. hybrid), another native of Australia, adds an unusual form to arrangements, and also dries well.

Trends

The latest materials to be air dried are slices of fruit – apples, oranges and lemons can be successfully air dried in a warm airing cupboard, if you are lucky enough to have one in your shop. Finally, encourage customers to bring their arrangements back regularly for cleaning, freshening up and maybe another lovely design.

Larkspur, artichokes, roses, statice and kangaroo paw are some of the air-dried materials seen here, ready for storage.

WEDDING FLOWERS

In the last hundred years, the wedding ceremony and bridal clothes have crystallized into a set of formal conventions, but within these limitations, there are still changes in fashion. The most popular colours for a wedding dress remain white, cream or ivory, while the bride's attendants are often dressed in shades of pink, blue, green, yellow and peach.

The style of bridal bouquets changes to mirror the era, varying from the large Edwardian bouquets of smilax, roses and carnations, to the sheaves of lilies carried over the arm in the 1930s, or the small stiff formal bouquets of the 1960s. In celebration of a united Europe, the European style of bouquet is now popular with many brides. This is smaller and more compact than the traditional British style. However it should not be formal and stiff, but have an elegance and movement.

To create successful wedding designs, it is essential to maintain an enlightened, receptive mind, willing to experiment with new ideas and concepts.

WEDDING DESIGNS

Weddings are gloriously busy and happy occasions, and one of the joys of being a florist is that you can be involved in the preparations for a wedding almost every week. The range of designs required for each wedding is wide, and this is one reason why the florist must have so many skills at her fingertips. The bride, bridesmaids, ushers, mums, relatives, church and reception – all these people and places will require flowers.

That said, weddings can be very simple affairs, and it is not unknown for the bride to pop into the florist just half an hour before the service. A pretty handtied bouquet is just right for such an occasion, and can be assembled very quickly. Generally, however, the bride and her mother, bridesmaids and groom will all arrive at the florist to discuss the choice of flowers and designs some months before the ceremony. The florist's role is to show the range of designs and blossoms that will be available when the wedding is to take place. Advice on individual preferences and colour choice is all part of the service.

Bridal bouquets must be carefully planned. If the flowers are to give their full value, the style of design, the materials being used, and their placement are important considerations. The flowers and foliage must be perfect and well-conditioned to withstand the rigours of the day.

When the wedding flowers arrive on the day, beautifully packaged, they will add that special touch to an occasion that would be incomplete without them. Today's bride walks in the footsteps of maidens of olden days who carried ears of wheat in their hands and 'corones' of flowers in their hair.

For the cake
This dainty all-round design, with its 'Jack Frost' roses and button chrysanthemums in a delicate wine glass, gives an attractive finishing touch to the wedding cake.

Handbag accessory
'Champagne' roses are combined with rich dark blue hyacinths and fragrant white freesias to make this a very special handbag accessory.

Shower bouquet
A pretty, natural design such as this shower, with its roses, freesias and carnation sprays, is given an individual touch with the addition of golden grasses.

Victorian posy
The cream 'Bahama' rose is the focal point of this charming design. The velvety African violets add a distinctive touch to the rich colourings of this appealing Victorian posy.

Pomander
This delightful little pomander has a lovely fragrance. Deep pink carnation sprays harmonize with flushed pink Viburnum carlesii, *and contrast with the blue hyacinths, and all are scented.*

A CARNATION BUTTONHOLE

A carnation buttonhole today is almost always a sign that a wedding is either about to take place or has just taken place. Years ago, it was commonplace to see a gentleman with a red carnation in the lapel of his jacket, inserted through the buttonhole into a specially-designed little glass or silver phial of water.

A carnation is still a very popular choice of buttonhole for both men and ladies, but nowadays white and pink are the colours most frequently ordered. There are many types of foliage that can be used, but *Asparagus setaceus* remains the most popular foliage for carnation buttonholes.

At weddings in the 1930s and 1940s, the bride's mother could be recognized by the number of carnations in her corsage – two or three at least, with plenty of fern and heavy tin foil. Today, carnation buttonholes are much more tailored, and green tape provides a discreet finish.

To make the buttonhole

If you have a large number of buttonholes to make, set up a mini production line rather than making each one individually. The method is the same for each, so you can save a lot of time this way.

Start by collecting together all the items required – carnations, *Asparagus setaceus*, wires, tape and pins. For each buttonhole, trim a carnation, leaving just a short length of stem; insert a 0.71mm (22 gauge) stub wire up the stem of the carnation, and make a closed hook, then pull the wire down until it is completely hidden in the base of the carnation flower.

Select three fronds of fern from the main shoot and mount them, using 0.32mm (30 gauge) silver stub wire. If the fern has stems of a reasonable length, it is not always necessary to mount them, and this can save much time.

After wiring, tape all the materials. Once the cut materials have all been prepared, they can then quickly be assembled into the buttonhole.

For assembly, add the fronds to the carnation, piece by piece. The largest frond is placed at the back, with a smaller frond at each side. The mounted fronds are flexible, and can be bevelled outwards at a becoming angle. Finally, add a pin.

1 *The carnation and fronds of* Asparagus sectaceus *are prepared by cutting stems to the correct length and then wiring. Use a 0.71mm (22 sgauge) stub wire for the carnation, and silver stub wire for foliage.*

2 *Tape the materials, using half-width tape for fern fronds and full width for the carnation. Arrange the fronds around the carnation, and firmly tape them in. Trim the wires to the required length.*

3 *The stem is covered with tape. A pin is added, and the carnation is sprayed with water. Other foliage can be used, including natural carnation foliage or ivy leaves; gypsophila makes a pretty alternative.*

A ROSE BUTTONHOLE

The romantic associations of the rose make it a popular choice for a buttonhole, and many grooms pick a rose of the same colour as those in the bridal bouquet. Roses can also be worn by the best man, the ushers and the lady guests.

The rose buttonhole is not exclusively used for weddings; it can be worn on formal or informal occasions, and is to be found on the lapels of suits in the city and in rural areas.

Florists today are fortunate in having a wide range of sizes and colours of rose from which to choose. A spray rose can make a tiny buttonhole for a child, while the sweetheart roses are a better size for a lady.

Making a rose buttonhole

Gather together all the materials – rose, stub wires, tape and pin. The rose has attractive foliage, so choose three perfect leaves.

Wire the cut materials. A rose with a stem of medium thickness will require a 0.71mm (22 gauge) wire, but you may need a heavier or lighter gauge of wire, depending on the weight of the rose. Insert the stub wire up the stem of the rose; it should be pushed just past the seed box.

The rose leaves need to be loop-stitched. A small stitch is taken at each side of the main vein, using 0.32mm (30 gauge) silver wire. Bring both ends of the wire down to the base of the leaf, at the back, supporting the stitch between finger and thumb to prevent the stitch from pulling. Secure the leaf stem and one of the wire ends by taking the remaining wire firmly around both, two or three times.

The rose and leaves are then taped. For ease of assembly, the leaves can be taped together, with the largest leaf in the middle, and a smaller one at each side.

For assembly, the rose is placed on top of the foliage; the largest leaf acts as a protective backing for the rose and also looks attractive. The buttonhole can be assembled either by using a short length of wire or with tape only. The wire stems are cut to length and then completely covered with tape. The design is sprayed with water and a pin added.

Rose foliage is the traditional backing, but as with the carnation, many other materials can be used, and a rose buttonhole for a lady is sometimes given a delicate ribbon bow for a finishing touch.

1 *Gather all the materials together. The rose and foliage are prepared; the rose has a wire inserted up the pre-cut stem, and the leaves are loop-stitched, using a 0.32mm (30 gauge) silver stub wire.*

2 *The lemon rose and the foliage are sealed, half-width tape being used for the foliage. The leaves can be taped together to make assembly easier. Cut the wires to the required length and seal with tape.*

3 *The assembled rose buttonhole is sprayed and a pin is added to complete the design; a pearl-headed pin can be used for a lady. This is a simple yet classic design, suitable for daytime or evening occasions.*

BUTTONHOLES

It is customary for the groom to pay for the flowers of the bride and bridesmaids, and sometimes included in this gift are flowers for the mothers of both the bride and groom, and also the groomsmen's buttonholes.

Carnations are frequently chosen, as they symbolize love and good luck, and the groom and best man often opt for red, the symbol for masculine love.

Many people now try to coordinate the flowers more fully, and instead of carnations they choose a flower included in the bride's bouquet. Sometimes, the groom alone will have a rose to match those in the bouquet, and everyone else will have carnations. This distinguishes the groom from the rest of the bridal party.

Buttonholes

These normally take the form of one large flower, such as a carnation or rose, with perhaps a small piece of foliage. The most popular foliage is *Asparagus setaceus*, but there is nothing wrong in using the natural foliage, such as rose or carnation leaves, or even hedera.

Boutonnieres

These are usually a bunch of small and dainty flowers grouped together – white heather, convalleria or stephanotis, for example.

Every wedding is individual, and as florists, we should surely encourage variety and small personal touches; this makes our jobs more interesting and each occasion unique and memorable.

Modern style
A very modern look is achieved by using a cream gerbera and bear grass. The design is finished off with a grouping of small cones and cream satin ribbon.

Carded buttonhole
White carnation buttonholes have always been popular for weddings. This is a carded buttonhole, the seed box and calyx having been removed to make the carnation sit flat. This type is often used for evenings, when it would be made without the fern.

Lucky heather

This wonderfully romantic sprig of lucky white heather is for the groom. Finished with a white satin bow, the design could also be worn by either a male or female guest.

Rose

The new varieties of rose are ideal for buttonholes, as they open fully to give impact, but do not shatter. The pink 'Jacaranda' rose is finished with a toning satin ribbon.

Orchid buttonhole

Orchids are a special flower, and ideal for a wedding. This pink cymbidium orchid is worn with a small piece of Hedera helix *and a pink bow.*

Lily

Something a little different – why not use a lily to match the bride's bouquet? This design is completed by adding variegated hedera and a sprig of broom.

CORSAGES

A corsage spray can be made from a wide range of fresh or dried flowers, foliage types, berries, seed heads and ribbons. These may be arranged into various styles, such as a posy, semi-crescent, crescent, or extension. Usually, a corsage is worn on the shoulder, but it can also be attached at the neck, waist, wrist or ankle.

The corsage spray is highly versatile, and can be adapted for many further uses – to decorate a hat, for example, or for a handbag, prayer book, parasol or fan. Discuss with your customers their preferences with regard to colours, types of flowers and use of ribbon. Some people expect ribbon to be included, while others do not; this might depend on local taste. A well-made design should have a flat back, an elevated profile with flowers and foliage on various levels, and all materials radiating from a focal point. Wiring must be discreet and, where possible, concealed, and this includes the binding point and stem end. The design should be lightweight and easy to attach. Suitable flowers include orchids, small lilies, freesias, car-nation sprays, hyacinths, stephanotis, nerines, bridal gladioli, and spray roses.

Loop stitch method for leaves

Remove most of the stem, leaving 6mm (¼in). Insert a fine silver wire in the back of the leaf, about one third from the tip and across the central vein. Make a small stitch. Pull both wires down at the base of the leaf; wind one wire around the stem and the other wire. Now tape to form a stem.

Method

Wire and tape all materials. Make two units of two leaves. Tape two roses together. Now place the leaf unit behind the roses. Next, bind in the main rose, gently easing it into a vertical position. Add two single leaves to each side of the main rose. Bind in single pieces of wax flower. To make the returned end, add the unit of two leaves and a piece of wax flower below the main flower. Add a bow. Trim out the excess wires and cut to the required length. Tape to form a stem; and finish with the pin.

1 *Hedera leaves are wired with the loop stitch method and taped to form a stem. The roses have been wired and taped, and both roses and leaves are taped into individual branching units.*

2 *Place a unit of hedera behind the rose unit, and bind them together with silver wire. Add the main rose and gently ease it into a vertical position. Bind in two leaves, one at each side of the main rose.*

The corsage spray is a very versatile design, as it can be worn or used to decorate a handbag, hat or other items.

HAT AND HANDBAG SPRAYS

These designs are a variation on the corsage spray, but in this case attached to a customer's hat or handbag. A traditional corsage spray is the design usually worn by most lady guests at a wedding. For the customer who requires something a little different, however, the type of design shown here offers an attractive alternative. Always ask to see the customer's hat or handbag, as you can then advise on the most suitable style of decoration and method of attachment. Carefully explain to your cus-

tomer the various methods of attaching the spray, and always gain her permission.

This type of design is particularly appropriate if the customer is wearing a highly patterned and brightly coloured dress on which flowers would not be seen, or if the dress is made of a lightweight fabric, so that pinning a corsage could be difficult and, worse still, might mark the fabric. The hat or bag should be brought to the shop a few days before the occasion, and carefully labelled and stored.

WHAT YOU WILL NEED

Wires, tape, ribbon, interesting flowers, such as orchids, gerberas, lilies, wax flowers and roses, and foliages, including eucalyptus, *Hedera helix*, *Skimmia japonica* and bear grass.

Method of attachment

For security, discreetly sew the spray to the hat. For a handbag, either tie the spray to the bag with ribbon, or use a taped, ribbon-covered wire, attaching the spray to the wire and then securing the wire ends together under the flap of the bag.

For this quick and easy-to-assemble design, wire and tape the single flower, foliage and ribbon loop. Construct the spray by binding leaves, wax flowers and ribbon loops under the main flower on several levels.

Two mini orchids with foliage make a simple hat spray: wire and tape materials; form the foliage into units; place an orchid among the foliage; add the second orchid and leaves; bind together, and tape to form the stem.

Completed designs are securely attached to the hat or handbag, ready for the special occasion.

HOOPS

A hoop is defined as a novelty design that can be carried by a bride, bridesmaid or flower girl. It would normally be carried by a small child, and there are many possible sizes and styles. The large hoop in the main picture shows the traditional way of decorating this design, but the one featured in the step photographs has been made in the modern style, to show how this differs.

Construction

The hoop is first covered with paper ribbon, which is simply wound around the hoop and held firmly at the join with florists' tape. The flowers are wired and taped, using the appropriate methods, and bound together with fine binding wire. The wires are divided into two sections and bent outwards after being trimmed to approximately 2.5cm (1in). They are then taped onto the hoop and the leaves pulled over the taping to conceal it.

Another way to make this type of design would be to make a garland and wind it around the hoop.

Choice of materials

Small dainty flowers are the most suitable for a hoop; large flowers are too heavy and would be difficult to balance. They would also be visually too heavy for such a dainty design.

As with any bridal design, the colours will be chosen to match the dresses of the bride and her bridesmaids, and the flowers to match the bride's bouquet. Ribbon trails may be used to complete the design.

WHAT YOU WILL NEED

Plastic-coated metal hoop, paper ribbon, roses, cymbidium orchids, bear grass, fatshedera leaves, stub wires, tape, and binding wire.

1 *The paper ribbon is unravelled and firmly attached at one end before being wound around the hoop to cover it.*

2 *The materials are wired and taped in the appropriate ways, and the spray is constructed and firmly attached to the hoop. The spray must be well balanced.*

The modern design is a little stark in comparison to the fluffy traditional hoop, but both have their place.

A PRAYER BOOK SPRAY

A prayer book decorated with a spray of flowers can be carried either by the bride or by a bridesmaid. You need to see the book to assess the size of floral spray required. The completed design must look attractive without overpowering the prayer book. Ask the bride to bring the book into the shop prior to the wedding. Wrap, label and store it carefully, as the item is of great sentimental value to the bride.

Assembly

Collect all the materials together and, working on a sheet of paper, prepare the ribbons (if required), and then the foliage and the flowers. This elongated style of corsage will require longer-than-usual units of flowers and foliage.

Assemble the corsage by binding units together under the focal flower. Use finer materials to create the outline, and position the main flowers in a curving line to establish the profile. Add the trailing units of flowers and foliage. Next, bind in single leaves and flowers on various levels and recess some materials. Now trim out excess wires; tape the stem end, and firmly wire the spray onto a 'figure-of-eight' wire foundation (see below).

Check that the book is the correct way up, then position the spray on the centre, bending the wire frame over the top and bottom edges of the book and clamping it firmly onto the inside cover.

Place the ribbon streamers where they can act as a page marker during the ceremony. Check the design; adjust the materials; carefully and lightly mist the spray; protect the book with paper, and store it in a cool place until it is required.

Attaching the spray

Using white tape, secure lengths of 0.71mm (22 gauge) wire together. Manipulate the wires to form a figure-of-eight, secured at the centre with binding wire. Cover the binding wire with white tape, and attach the spray to the foundation at the central point.

The spray can be sewn or glued to the ribbon; alternatively, a purpose-made plastic clip, at the centre of which are two wires with which to attach the spray, can be slid onto the cover of the book.

WHAT YOU WILL NEED

Main flowers (roses, orchids, small lilies, mini-gerberas), transitional flowers (freesias, bridal gladioli, hyacinths, stephanotis, alstroemeria, nerines, convallaria, spray roses, Singapore orchids, hellebores), foliage (jasmine, nephrolepis, wax flower, soft ruscus, eucalyptus, hedera), wires, tapes and ribbons.

1 *Prepare all the materials. This design is assembled in the same way as a corsage – the roses form the main line, and trailing units of materials add length to the design.*

2 *To attach the spray to the book, make a figure-of-eight wire frame. The spray is attached at the central point and the wire frame is then bent over the cover of the book.*

The larger prayer book spray is to be carried by the bride, and the smaller version by her bridesmaid.

A COMB HEADDRESS

This headdress is individually designed as an accessory for the bride or for a bridesmaid or guest. It is another variation on the corsage, and is made to complement the bridal bouquet. The design might be formed with a single flower or made from several small blossoms.

Materials chosen for this, as for any type of headdress, must be durable. The head is a warm part of the body, and fresh flowers must be able to withstand this heat for several hours (a flower sealant can be used to prevent flowers transpiring). Shorter, flatter types of flower, such as carnation sprays, gerberas, roses and single chrysanthemum sprays, are generally best. Weight is another factor to be considered – bride and bridesmaids will forget they are even wearing a design that is feather light. The comb headdress also has the advantage of being suitable for either short or long hair; extra hair grips can be used for very fine hair.

The finished design can either be glued to the comb or attached with a well-taped 0.56mm (24 gauge) wire. Ensure that the wire ends are safely finished underneath the corsage, and not on the side of the comb next to the head.

WHAT YOU WILL NEED

A comb, muscari, Hedera helix, carnation spray, a small amount of variegated grass, and a selection of wires and tapes.

The flowers and foliage are first prepared with the lightest support wires and half-width tape. They are then arranged into a design which is similar in style to a corsage.

The completed design is attached to the comb with a taped 0.56mm (24 gauge) stub wire, both ends of the wire being safely returned to the corsage side of the comb, away from the wearer's head.

Two attractive hair accessories have been designed to complement the dress and flowers of bride or bridesmaids.

GARLAND HEADDRESS

1 *The headdress is constructed on millinery wire, cut to the correct length and taped to form a circle. The flowers and foliage are wired on 0.32mm (30 gauge) wires, and neatly taped.*

2 *All materials are taped firmly onto the millinery wire, with tape cut to a width of 12mm (½in). The silver wires are trimmed out during construction to make the design less bulky.*

T he bride's headdress completes her whole outfit, and should therefore complement the bouquet. Many brides are concerned that the flowers will not last, and they therefore steer away from fresh flowers; this is such a pity, as fresh flowers always look wonderful, and if suitable flowers are chosen they will have the advantage of matching the bouquet and will certainly look much lovelier than artificial ones.

Flowers such as stephanotis, Singapore orchids, cymbidium orchids, gypsophila, spray carnations and even many varieties of rose would be appropriate, as would foliage such as hedera or eucalyptus.

WHAT YOU WILL NEED

Roses, spray carnations, gypsophila, foliage (such as euonymus or hedera), tape, millinery wire, and 0.32mm (30 gauge) stub wires.

Style of headdress

It is important, when helping a bride to select a headdress, to apply certain rules. As with the bouquet, the headdress must link with the dress style, fabric and colour, and also with the bridal bouquet. It must also be suitable for the bride's hair style. It is no good to choose a comb or slide fitting if the bride has short silky hair through which it would slip. The design must suit the shape of the bride's face, her type of hair, and also her hair style.

Types of headdress

The most popular type of headdress is the garland or circlet. It can be made any width, to suit the person wearing it, and from flowers ranging from gypsophila and other dainty flowers, for a child bridesmaid, to large roses, lilies and even amaryllis, the latter for the bride with a taste for the dramatic. The benefit of the garland design is that it is easy to wear, will not slip out of the hair, and it suits most types of hair style.

If a full garland is felt to be inappropriate, an Alice band is a good alternative. Again, it is easy to wear, especially for small children who have fine silky hair.

Another option is a comb or slide, onto which a corsage type of design is attached. The veil is sometimes attached to the comb.

This beautiful garland headdress in peach and cream would be a crowning glory for any bride.

AN ALICE BAND HEADDRESS

Being able to offer a selection of head-dresses to a bride is part of a florist's expertise. The Alice band style makes an attractive alternative to the circlet or garland headdress, and is particularly useful if a bridesmaid has fine, silky hair. Soft thin elastic is threaded through a slot at each end of the band and is taken under the hair at the back of the head, holding the band in position.

WHAT YOU WILL NEED

Glue gun and glue, fine silver wires, tape, plastic Alice band, and a combination of flowers, various types of foliage and, if desired, ribbon bows.

Always obtain the head measurement, so the design can be made to the appropriate length. Remember, where possible, to link the colours and types of materials used in the headdress with those being carried. Use good quality, well-conditioned flowers and foliage; it is important to use materials with lasting qualities, as much body heat is lost through the head.

With practice, this attractive headdress is quick and easy to assemble, as the only materials which need to be prepared are the ribbon bows, but the glue gun must be handled with care.

Simple construction

Switch on the glue gun and place your materials on a sheet of paper. Prepare small ribbon bows and wire and tape small clusters of wax flowers, removing most of the flower stems. Starting at the ends of the headband, glue on first a small trail of hedera and then an attractive combination of flowers and ribbons. Work from the ends up to the centre and then fill any gaps with small flowers or clusters of foliage. Allow the glue to dry completely; spray the finished band lightly with water, and store. For safety reasons, do not forget to switch off the glue gun if it is not required for further use!

1 *The dainty ribbon bows and clusters of wax flowers are wired and taped. Most of the flower stems are removed. Starting at each end of the band, glue the individual flowers, leaves and bows of ribbon into place.*

2 *Continue gluing materials to each side of the band. Work towards the centre, making sure that flowers, foliage and ribbons overlap, and materials are placed on all levels. Fill in any gaps with small flowers, and ensure that all materials are secure.*

The Alice band is now covered with materials and the headdress is ready to wear. The small groupings of materials in front of the headdress show the scale of flowers and foliage used.

BRIDESMAID'S POSY

The bridesmaids' flowers should never overshadow those of the bride, so the design should be smaller in size than the bride's bouquet. The colours are normally chosen to match the dresses of the bride and bridesmaids, and the bridesmaids will often carry more brightly coloured flowers than those in the bridal bouquet.

The posy has always been a popular design, partly because the size can be altered to suit the age and height of each bridesmaid. Until recent years, the posy would have been wired, but with the development of foam posy holders, the process has been simplified.

Certain flowers have always been popular for wedding designs; these include roses, spray carnations, freesias and Singapore orchids. The wax flower, which is relatively new to floristry work, is also ideal, as it is both dainty and long lasting.

WHAT YOU WILL NEED

Roses, spray carnations, *Helleborus niger*, wax flower, *Hedera helix* 'Glacier', and a foam posy holder.

1 *The holder is dipped into water for a minute or two before being used. A circular outline is formed with foliage.*

2 *A main line of five roses is added to the design, the centre rose being the tallest; other materials are then added at different heights to build up the profile. Spray carnations are added as a secondary flower.*

This lovely posy, with its vibrant colours, would complement any bridesmaid's outfit.

VICTORIAN POSY

I t was in the middle years of the nine-teenth century that the Victorian posy became a favourite with both bride and bridesmaid. The design remained popular until the end of the century, when the show-er bouquet took its place as the most favoured style.

The Victorian posy invariably has a rose in the centre as the focal flower. The circles of flowers surrounding the rose can be made with any small flower that has a flat or rounded head. In this design, scented hyacinths and scarlet carnation sprays are used with *Viburnum carlesii*, which adds

WHAT YOU WILL NEED

A single rose, *Viburnum carlesii*, carnation spray, hyacinth pips, *Skimmia japonica* 'Rubella', *Camellia japonica* (for edging and backing the posy), bear grass, ribbon (for a bow and to com-plete the handle), and tapes and wires.

another texture and its own light fragrance.

A design of this type is shaped in a soft dome, and the outer row of flowers are often a spike form, such as sprigs of heather, lilies of the valley or, as here, flowers of *Skimmia japonica* 'Rubella'.

The posy can be completed with a circle of foliage or a pretty lace frill. In many cases, a combination of both is appealing

(see page 143). The pointed leaves of the camellia are used in this design, the glossy surface of the foliage contrasting well with the other textures.

This design has been given a further dimension with the addition of an extension, constructed out of bear grass, with a green annealed 0.90mm (20 gauge) wire concealed underneath. The taped extension wire is attached at the binding point. Small reversed camellia leaves give a neat finish to the design. A small grouping of flowers and foliage are neatly wired, taped and attached to the grass.

1 *The rose and other flowers that need support are taped, as is the camellia. Aside from the rose, materials on the inner part of the posy do not require taping.*

2 *The rose and the viburnum are bound together, using fine silver wire. Carnation sprays of even size are then taken around the posy.*

3 *As flowers are added, it is important to bevel them gently to achieve the requisite soft dome shape characteris-tic of this posy.*

4 *The binding is clearly seen. Camellia leaves are added for the edg-ing and extension, and are reversed at the back to hide the mechanics.*

The Victorian posy is as captivating today as it was in the nineteenth century.

SEASONAL HANDTIED BOUQUETS

I t is all too easy for a florist to use similar combinations of all-year-round flowers on a regular, and perhaps monotonous, basis, but you can just as easily give your bouquets the flavour of passing seasons.

The bouquets pictured here were each made with a particular time of year in mind, and one example was made to suggest a particular month.

Handtied designs are becoming widely accepted by the public. Surveys suggest that customers, when given the choice, come out in favour of the instant appeal of immediately accessible flowers. It has not, however, been so easy to persuade florists to opt for handtied bouquets, which require extra skills that are not needed for a bouquet wrapped in cellophane.

Handtied bouquets have gained popularity with brides, who appreciate their Edwardian feel (note how *Asparagus plumosus* is making a comeback after several years during which gypsophila has been the favourite). The most recent handtied fashion is the waterfall, in which flowers cascade downwards. This can either be held over one arm or to the front, in much the same way as a shower bouquet.

Summer waterfall
This waterfall bouquet would be a lovely design for a summer bride to carry. Roses, larkspurs, freesias and broom combine with the delicate fronds of Asparagus plumosus.

Scented springtime
Spring tulips, 'Bridal Crown' narcissi, and spring foliage mix with all-year-round roses and wax flowers to make a charming and delicately-scented design.

Winter bouquet

Cream roses and orange
clivia give warmth to this winter
bouquet. Euphorbia, cotoneaster
berries and tight buds of viburnum
make an interesting blend of
materials.

Spring bride

This handtied bunch of lilies of the
valley brings the freshness of spring to
mind. The fragrance is one of the
loveliest floral scents, light and delicate,
just like the flowers.

Shades of autumn

Autumn colours make appealing
blends, and here the oats and dark
beech leaves provide a strong contrast
to the vibrant oranges and reds of the
roses, lilies and alstroemerias.

A STRAIGHT SHOWER BOUQUET

This style of design is defined as a formal bouquet, and the construction incorporates a handle, which allows the bouquet to be carried easily at either a wedding or a formal presentation. Flowers, foliage and accessories are arranged in specific styles, such as a straight shower, as seen here, a semi-crescent, or line. The traditional method of assembly is to wire and mount all the materials, with the wires forming the handle. The modern approach is to use a wet or dry foam bouquet holder.

Foam holders

If you are using a foam holder, use fresh, good quality, well-conditioned materials. Cut the stems to an arrow point – in other words, with sharp angles on both sides – and avoid using materials with thick or fleshy stems. Add glue to the stems to give extra security; long or brittle stems can be support-wired.

Collect all your materials and secure the foam holder in a bouquet stand. Create the outline by inserting foliage into the foam, near the holder. Add short stems of foliage to the top of the holder to hide the foam. Place focal flowers down the centre line of the bouquet, raising the main flower to create the profile.

Strengthen the outline with bud materials, and fill in by adding lines and groupings of flowers and foliage. Place single flowers and leaves on various levels to complete the profile, recessing some to give visual depth. To check the visual balance, shape and profile, hold the bouquet in front of a mirror, making adjustments if necessary. Finally, spray each section of the bouquet. Pack it carefully in an air-tight box and store it in a cool place until required.

WHAT YOU WILL NEED

Lilies – as the main flowers, transitional forms (freesias, narcissi, carnation sprays, roses), materials to create the outline (Singapore orchids and ruscus), foam bouquet holder, bouquet stand, and support wires and glue gun, if required.

1 *Until you can confidently construct a bouquet, always lay the materials out on a work top to help you to create the correct shape and gauge the ideal position for the flowers. The overall size of a bouquet is approximately a third of the bride's height, but a flowing dress could demand a larger bouquet.*

2 *First, use foliage to create the pear-shaped outline, then place a line of graded focal flowers down the centre, with the main flower in the centre.*

3 *The foliage outline is now linked to the focal flowers, with bud materials at the outer edges and larger flowers and foliage at the centre.*

For many brides, the full classical straight shower style is the perfect wedding bouquet.

A LINE BOUQUET

Perhaps the easiest style of bouquet to make, this requires only a limited number of flowers, foliage types and, if desired, ribbon. This basic bouquet is the foundation of other styles, such as the straight shower.

Constructing the bouquet

Collect together all the materials and equipment. Work on a sheet of paper. First make a ribbon bow for the handle, and two other four-loop bows for the bouquet. Prepare the foliage by support wiring, if necessary, then mount and tape the stems.

Lay the main flowers out on the workbench. Carefully cut them to the required length, and then support wire, mount and tape them. Next, wire and mount the secondary materials.

Start to assemble the bouquet, beginning with the longest foliage units (here, bear grass) and flowers (gerberas). Bend the mount wires at a 45 degree angle to form the handle, and bind them together. Bind in the main focal flower in a raised position to form an elevated profile, and add a fifth gerbera in an upright position. Next, add secondary materials in diagonal lines and recess a bow at each side of the focal flower.

To finish, trim excess wires from the handle and cut to 13.75cm (5½in). Add the bow and cover the handle with white tape. Take ribbon on a roll and hold it behind the binding point of the handle, leaving a streamer; take it down behind the handle and up to the front, covering the handle tip; bind the handle from top to bottom, carefully covering the tip again, and wind ribbon back up to the binding point. Cut the ribbon, again leaving a streamer, and firmly tie both streamers behind and in front of the bow.

WHAT YOU WILL NEED

Bold flowers on natural stems (such as gerberas, roses or double tulips), bear grass or hedera, *Nephrolepis exaltata*, convallaria, muscari, ixia, gaultheria flower spikes, a selection of wires, tape, ribbons to blend, and a bouquet stand.

1 *Gerberas are cut to the required length, support wired, mounted and taped, and bear grass is mounted to form trailing units and loops. Gaultheria and* Nephrolepis exaltata *are mounted in single and double units.*

2 *Position the gerberas to form a strong visual line. Units of bear grass add length. Bend mount wires at a 45 degree angle and bind at one point, forming the handle.*

3 *To strengthen the main line, add lines of secondary materials, radiating from the main focal flower. Always keep to the original binding point.*

This simple but effective bouquet is now ready to be carried by a bride or, as here, by a bridesmaid.

BASKETS FOR WEDDINGS

Flowers and foliage attractively arranged in baskets make lovely designs for bridesmaids and flower girls to carry at a wedding.

Easy to carry, such baskets are ideal for small children to hold. If the flowers and foliage are arranged at several levels and for all-round viewing, a design of this type will always look quite charming in wedding photographs, however awkwardly a young child may hold it.

Seasonal variations

A basket can be designed to reflect a particular season and will look delightful, for example, when filled with spring flowers, such as tulips, hyacinths, freesias, muscari and narcissi. For the summer months, you might combine larkspur, sweet peas, scabious, pinks, cornflowers and roses. Wheat, corn, berries, seed heads, copper beech, roses and lilies are appropriate for an autumn wedding; while the winter bridesmaid might bear a rustic basket filled with variegated hedera, blue pine, conifer, holly, heathers, roses, freesias and Euphorbia fulgens.

For presentation

During the wedding reception, many newly married couples wish to thank their parents publicly. A basket of flowers and foliage is a perfect gift for several reasons: as the flowers and foliage are arranged in water-retaining foam, they will remain fresh throughout the reception, which is particularly useful if it is an evening function; a basket is also easy to present, carry and transport home. If the basket is to be a memento, suggest that it is returned to the shop and filled with fabric and dried flowers echoing those used in the bride's bouquet. This is a lovely keepsake, especially for the bride's mother.

Memento basket
Dried and fabric materials, similar to those in the bridal bouquet, have been arranged in a basket which will be perfect for presentation and will make a lovely memento of a happy day.

For a young child

Even a very small child could manage this tiny rustic basket, filled with dainty roses, button chrysanthemum sprays, freesia, and a range of foliage types.

Designed for impact
This striking basket makes an impressive presentation, and can include a variety of flowers and foliage types, to suit any colour combination.

Bridesmaid's baskette
A baskette is a contrived design – all materials are wired, taped and formed into units, and then bound together to form this basket-like design.

Thank-you basket
For presentation to the mothers of the bride and groom, this low, flowing arrangement of flowers and different types of foliage makes this style of basket the ideal way of saying' Thank you'.

A EUROPEAN BOUQUET

This bouquet made in the European style is dramatic, elegant, and would certainly be suitable for the bride who wants something unusual. This type of design is very popular in competition work, but as yet is not readily accepted by the general public. It is ideal for a registry office wedding, when perhaps the bride is wearing a suit or similar less formal outfit, but with a traditional full-skirted wedding dress most people still prefer a full shower or a tied-over-the-arm design.

WHAT YOU WILL NEED

Stem lilies, roses, rubus foliage, bear grass, contorted willow, hyacinth, hebe foliage, foam holder, and glue.

Construction

The bouquet shown is made in a small foam holder; if too much foam is used, it is difficult to cover, and this also applies to modern flower arrangements. The shape is angular, with stark bold materials used in strong groupings. This design has great flexibility and can be very appealing.

Blossom, berries or mosses are recessed very low into the design to give weight and depth to the centre. These materials also cover up the foam. Large bold flowers are used to give the main vertical placement; fine materials are added to one side, and these are balanced on the other side by shorter heavier materials. The secondary flowers, such as roses, freesia, stephanotis or convallaria, are then added.

1 *A vertical placement of contorted willow and lilies is used to achieve height. The proportions are ⅜ up and ⅝ down, rather than ⅓ and ⅔, as in a traditional bouquet.*

2 *Width is achieved through the use of large leaves and a line of roses, and height by using contorted willow. Stems must be secured firmly into the foam, which can be achieved by gluing.*

A truly dramatic bouquet of peach lilies, roses and navy blue hyacinths.

STRUCTURED BOUQUETS

These stylish bouquets have a natural grace and elegance that can either be tailored and refined or can express an unpretentious simplicity. They offer the bride an alternative design to the traditional showers and the somewhat countrified tied bouquets.

For the repeat bride (a term that some prefer to use), a daintier and more sophisticated bouquet is often preferred. The flowers may be teamed with an elegant dress or suit. The colours and textures of cut materials should harmonize with the fabric of the dress. A large and flowing bouquet would be unsuitable on this occasion and would certainly obscure the dress.

Construction techniques

Structured bouquets are constructed in a similar way to those in the traditional style, but the design is different, and the bouquet sits on top of the hand rather than being held facing forwards in the hand. Space, and the texture and groupings of flowers are important. Foliage has an integral role, and berries, cones and even stems play a part in these designs, which look attractive from all angles, with special cut materials at the back of the design for the bride to enjoy. Guests can admire the bride's wedding ring, as the bouquet allows the hand to be seen.

The structured bouquet is not only seen at weddings, but is also a suitable design for presentations at any time of the day or evening, on the many occasions where fresh flowers can complete a special event.

A bow of lilies

A very special design for a bride or a bridesmaid. New Zealand flax is looped in a bow effect that creates a visual tie between the liatris and pale pink 'La Rêve' lilies. Misty grey foliage gives the design distinctive lines and strong groupings.

Summer bride

This peaches and cream bouquet, with lime-green Alchemilla mollis, would be a lovely bouquet for a summer bride. The berries of the Gaultheria shallon hint at the approaching autumn.

Tangy autumn

A spicy-coloured lily, orange roses, tangerine carnations and warm russet freesia contrast sharply with the shiny dark beech leaves.

Tailored elegance

The striking use of the ferns, rolled bergenia leaves and lemon calla lilies in this delicately coloured bouquet make it an ideal choice for a bride wearing a tailored suit at a civil wedding.

Sweet spring

Spring is in the air with this bouquet of scented hyacinths and cream roses and lilies. The variegated grass gives a spiky contrast to the softer curves and rounds of the other foliage.

PACKING WEDDING FLOWERS

As the time for the wedding draws near, the bride's home will be full to overflowing with relatives, friends and perhaps neighbours, and the florist can be sure of some appreciative oohs and ahhs when the flowers are delivered, especially if they have been specially packaged.

When you have taken so much care with the preparation and designing of the wedding flowers, it is worth paying some attention to the presentation of the designs.

Packaging practicalities

In addition to its impact value, packaging has other positive and practical advantages for the florist. The tissue paper should be printed with your business name, so that everyone can see where the flowers were designed, with your business address and telephone number, for ease of contact.

Quite apart from the advertizing value of the packaging, the enclosing cellophane will protect the flowers from extremes of temperature while they are being transported to the bride's home, and will help to create the moist microclimate that is essential if the flowers are to remain in tiptop condition until they are needed. Good packaging is inexpensive in both cost and time, and its benefits are more than just oohs and ahhs.

WHAT YOU WILL NEED

A sturdy flower box, lengths of tissue paper (printed with your business name and telephone number), firm cellophane, and staples or cellotape.

1 A wedding box can be made in several ways; here, an empty flower box is covered with tissue paper and a hole is made for the stem of the bouquet, with a collar of tissue to support the flowers.

2 The bouquet can be laid gently onto the tissue collar. The other designs are added, with a little cellotape to prevent them from sliding around. The cellophane is taken over the entire box.

The cellophane is folded and fixed at each corner, so that it stands above the bouquet without touching the flowers.

SYMPATHY TRIBUTES

Sympathy flowers form an emotional link between the living and the deceased. They are a way of expressing grief and help people to mourn. Designs have become more informal, perhaps reflecting today's lifestyle. There is often a request for family flowers only, or for donations; this may be due partly to the cost of flowers as well as to changing attitudes.

It is very important that flowers, if they are sent, should be of excellent quality and beautifully presented. All designs should be well constructed with fresh good quality flowers; wilting, over-mature flowers or badly constructed designs are not acceptable.

Funeral work has changed dramatically in recent years due to the introduction of plastic foam, which has speeded up the process of construction by doing away with the mossing of bases and wiring of flowers. Most flowers have also been developed to last much longer now than ever before.

SYMPATHY DESIGNS

Sympathy flowers bear an important role in the grieving process. Studies show that flowers, which are sent as expressions of grief, support and respect, offer a genuine comfort, both to the bereaved and to those sending tributes.

Professional florists have a responsibility to provide high-quality floral tributes. The cut materials used should be fresh, at the appropriate stage of maturity, and mechanically stable and capable of withstanding considerable amounts of handling.

Flowers can be sent either to the home of the deceased or to the chapel of the funeral director. In both cases, it is important that cards are clearly and neatly written, with the name and service details on the back. A brief description of the type and nature of the tribute is also helpful.

Deliveries

Ensure that deliveries are carried out in a respectful and professional manner – there should be no impression of a last-minute rush. Containers should not leak, and designs must be stable and well balanced. Pollen stains are difficult to eradicate, so stamens should be removed from lilies.

Prickly and sharp foliages should be avoided, as they make tributes tiresome and difficult for funeral directors to handle.

Sheaf

Arum lilies (Zantedeschia aethiopica) *are here combined with* Euphorbia marginata, Arum italicum *and eucalyptus foliage. The selection of foliage types complements the arums beautifully.*

A formal posy

Often called a posy pad, a dainty design such as this would be a suitable tribute for a child. Here, lemon roses have been teamed with muscari and micro-gerberas.

Informal open heart

This popular design contains a selection of yellow, cream and white flowers, arranged to emphasize the heart shape of the tribute.

Wreath

This appealing and attractive wood-land wreath features eye-catching clusters of spring flowers and foliage. Alder catkins harmonize with the mossy base and evergreen foliage.

Coffin spray

This magnificent spray includes some very lovely, choice flowers, all of them white. The strong grey foliage sets off the white flowers and also acts as protection for the more delicate blooms.

PREPARING A MOSSED FRAME

Most florists use plastic foam bases as foundations for funeral tributes, as preparing a moss frame – mossing the frame, backing and then edging it – is a tedious task. However, the techniques involved in using a mossed frame are part of the florist's basic skills.

Mossing, backing and edging

Collect the materials together and start by cleaning the damp moss, removing any twigs or stones. Attach reel wire or string to the frame and, with the frame directly in front of you, place several handfuls of moss, about 5cm (2in) high, on the frame. Bind the moss on firmly, and continue, adding moss evenly and binding diagonally across the fame until it is completely covered with moss. Take the reel wire around for a sec-ond time between the previous twists of wire. Cut the wire; return it into the moss, and trim the moss to an even shape.

Now back the wreath: turn the frame over; secure the wreath wrap with hairpins on the inside; stretch the wrap over the frame and hairpin it in place at regular inter-vals. Continue the process until the frame is complete.

Finally, the wreath must be edged. Double-leg mount well-balanced fans of cupressus (see page 51) and, starting on the outer edge, insert the wired fans into the lower part of the frame, just on the wreath wrap. The anchored foliage should slope downwards, towards the workbench. Complete first the outer and then the inner edges, ensuring that the foliage overlaps and maintaining an even circular shape.

WHAT YOU WILL NEED

Damp clean moss, teased out into small piles, wire frame, 0.56mm (24 gauge) reel wire or string, wreath wrap, 0.90mm (20 gauge) x 180mm (7½in) stub wires, and German pins or hairpins made of 0.90mm (20 gauge) wire.

---

1 *Handfuls of damp moss are firmly attached to the frame with reel wire or string. When the whole frame has been mossed, it should have a good shape, with a firm, even finish, and it should not be too heavy.*

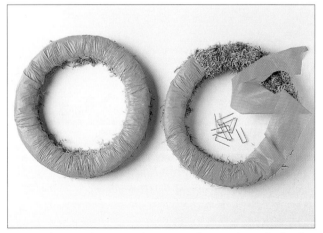

2 *Wreath wrap is hairpinned securely to the back of the frame. The backing provides a professional finish; gives protection; hides the wires, and helps to retain moisture.*

3 *Fans of cupressus are anchored securely, low down around the inner and outer edges of the frame. The completed edging protects the flowers and also gives an attractive border to the tribute.*

A FOAM FRAME

To prepare a foam frame, first chamfer the edge of the foam, using a sharp knife and removing approximately 12mm (½in) of foam. Carefully smooth off the chamfered edge with your hand, to round off the edges. Removing the right-angled edge assists you to achieve the required bevelled effect. When basing a tribute such as a chaplet, wreath or open heart, however, remember not to remove the edge of the foam at the place where the plastic bump for the spray or cluster will be secured to the frame.

Various edgings can be glued, pinned or wired to the base. Strong-stemmed foliage, such as cupressus, can simply be pushed firmly into the foam. Single leaves give a tailored finish to a tribute. Use bold foliage, such as laurel, camellia, *Hedera helix canariensis*, *Elaeagnus pungens* 'Maculata', eucalyptus, or *Skimmia japonica*.

Edging with single leaves
Soak the frame lightly and select graded mature leaves (new foliage is soft and will wilt quickly). Avoid using damaged or misshapen leaves. Clean the leaves, removing dirt and dust. For extra support and control, loop stitch each leaf, using the support wire as a mount. Starting at a point, firmly insert a wired small leaf. This will accentuate the point. Now work to the centre of the frame, overlapping leaves slightly. Return to a point, and repeat the process until the edging is complete. Ensure that you maintain the exact shape of the pillow.

Lightly spray the edged frame with leaf cleaner, to give a polished finish.

WHAT YOU WILL NEED

Foam based tribute, sharp knife, single leaves, stub wires, and leaf shine.

1 *At the top is a prepared frame. Below is a frame of the same type, but the top and one side have been chamfered with a sharp knife and the edge gently rounded. Lightly soak the chamfered frame.*

2 *Clean and undamaged single leaves are wired and firmly inserted around the edge to establish the outline. When the edging is complete, the distinctive pillow shape is still retained.*

RIBBON EDGING

R ibbon edging is a versatile addition for both formal and informal tributes. Ribbon can complement both based and open designs, and it can harmonize or provide contrast and add texture to funeral designs.

There are two types of pleating – box pleats and overlapping pleats. Box pleats are made by folding the ribbon first one way and then in the opposite direction. For overlapping pleats, the ribbon is folded in the same direction throughout. Whichever method is chosen, the folds must be orderly and equal.

A hand stapler is used to fasten the ribbon, and either German pins or the glue gun to fix the ribbon to the tribute. Corners are mitred to give a very neat finish to tributes such as the cushion, heart and cross. Ribbon used for the edging can be employed in the tribute, in the form of loops and trails, to create a sense of complete unity.

WHAT YOU WILL NEED

A selection of ribbons to complement the flower and foliage materials, a hand-held staple gun, German pins or a glue gun, and a prepared tribute – either mossed or on a foam base.

---

1 *This stiff paper ribbon has been box pleated in two sections. Beginning at the point of the heart, where a straight piece of ribbon is left for the mitring, the ribbon is pinned or glued in place.*

2 *An overlapping pleat is used for this tribute, ribbon being left at the point, for mitring. The flow of the pleats will reverse direction so that they work towards the point of the heart.*

3 *Mitre the ribbon at the point by stapling the two ends together from underneath. At the top of the heart, the ribbon can be cut neatly at the indentation or brought a short way onto the frame.*

The wide range of ribbons now available makes it possible to give each of these tributes a different and interesting finish.

AN OPEN WREATH

The wreath represents the circle of life, and it was the Greeks and Romans who first used this symbol at funerals. Every rich Greek household employed a wreath maker to create the garlands, chaplets and wreaths that were used for decorations and awards as well as at funerals.

The open wreath is a popular design, with the public and florists alike. The variety of flower forms, textures and colour combinations ensure that this is an interesting and challenging design to make, and seasonal flowers can make it relatively inexpensive.

Carnations were chosen as the main or focal flowers for the wreath featured here. They are spaced regularly around the wreath, and interspersed with micro-gerberas. The spiky petals and daisy centre of the latter provide a contrast in form to the carnations. The gerberas were inserted in between the carnations, at a slightly lower level. Alstroemerias, which contrast in form with both the carnations and the gerberas, were placed in the inner circle and the outer circle, at different levels.

> ## WHAT YOU WILL NEED
>
> **A foam frame – lightly soaked, carnations, micro-gerberas, alstroemerias, *Viburnum tinus*, cupressus, and green 0.71mm (22 gauge) stub wires.**

To add to the textures in the wreath, *Viburnum tinus*, a very versatile evergreen foliage, was used to fill in any small spaces. The rosettes of dark green foliage and the tiny bronze buds and white flowers add another dimension to this open wreath. The combination of bold and warm oranges and reds make this a suitable colouring for a cold, and perhaps bleak, winter service.

Flowers are a comfort and act as a focus at funerals, when conversation can become difficult. Funeral directors are in a unique position to observe the effect of flowers at funerals, and many agree that the bereaved mention flowers as a comforting aspect of the funeral.

Companies sending flowers to a funeral service as a mark of respect will invariably choose a wreath as the traditional and more formal way of expressing sympathy.

1 *Cupressus is inserted around the inner and outer edges, keeping the distinctive shape. Extra foliage is added to the top of the frame.*

2 *The carnations are externally supported with green 0.71mm (22 gauge) wires. They, and the gerberas, are evenly spaced around the base.*

3 *Alstroemeria flowers and buds are inserted in the inner and outer circles. Support wires can be used for the vulnerable outer flowers.*

The warm, glowing reds and oranges make an attractive combination with the dark greens of the foliage.

OPEN/LOOSE TRIBUTE

The term open, or loose, describes the open construction of a tribute, using flowers of one or several types, in which foliage can be incorporated. These tributes can be made either of materials of one colour – tints, tones and shades of yellow, for example – or of any colour combination preferred by the customer.

Flowers and foliage can be freely arranged or used in patterns or groupings, but the materials are not bonded tightly together, as in a formal tribute. However, it is essential to retain the distinctive outline.

Various sizes of cross, heart, pillow, cushion and wreath can be constructed in either the formal style (see pages 203–209) or in the loose/open style. Many customers prefer the latter, more natural style of tribute, which emphasizes the individual shapes of the flowers, making all materials clearly visible.

Materials

The selection of materials is important. Use good quality, well-conditioned, mature flowers at their peak of perfection in colour and form. Avoid using tight buds, as they are too small and lack impact.

This design can look very attractive if made with seasonal flowers, such as the tulips, irises, narcissi and hyacinths of spring. Alternatively, a beautiful tribute might be designed with just one type of flower – a heart of open pink roses, interspersed with grey foliage, can express many feelings for a grieving customer. Fans of cupressus, single leaves or pleated ribbon edgings can provide attractive outlines, and a range of decorative types of foliage can be incorporated.

General method of construction

Space the main flowers evenly, on the same level – usually at the centre. Add secondary flowers to form the outline and fill in the design. Finally, intersperse the flowers with groups of foliage. As with all funeral tributes, remember to give the design a bevelled profile; place materials on all levels, and ensure that the overall height does not exceed 20–23cm (8–9in).

Open heart

An attractive alternative to a solid heart, this open frame is edged with single leaves. Mature roses are used as main flowers – carnations, lilies, narcissi, hellebores and variegated conifers fill in the design.

Solid heart – open style

This sounds like a contradiction in terms. However, the mature flowers and various types of foliage are freely arranged while the distinctive heart shape is retained.

Open wreath

Available in various sizes, this very versatile style of tribute can incorporate seasonal flowers or a combination of prestigious materials, while a pleated ribbon edge adds a distinctive finish.

Cross

This tribute can be made in a wide range of sizes, from a small cross to a full-scale coffin cross. Here, the design is outlined in cupressus; pale colours are used towards the outer edge, with richer colours at the centre emphasizing the cross symbol.

SINGLE AND DOUBLE SPRAYS

This informal tribute uses materials on natural stems, which can be wired for support and control when necessary. The materials are arranged in a variety of bases, including moss foundations and, even more frequently, plastic spray trays. Foliage such as Tsuga pine or *Abies grandis* is used to create a good outline, and almost any combination of flowers might be used. Suggest this type of design to the customer who wishes to send a tribute as a token of sympathy, perhaps for a neighbour or a distant relative.

Method of construction

Collect all the materials and prepare the base by gluing a third of a brick of foam into the tray and then securing it with pot tape. Soak the foam briefly in water. If you are using a prepared spray tray with handle, just soak it in water for several minutes.

With the handle facing you, create a pear-shaped outline by inserting the foliage low down in the foam. The rounded end covers the handle. The main focal flower, which is also the tallest and is single-leg mounted for security, is placed two-thirds down the foam. Other focal flowers may be wired and mounted if necessary. Starting at the outline, add flowers in a diagonal line – buds at the outer edge and open flowers in the centre.

Add flowers and foliage on all levels, making an elevated profile. Recess some shorter-stemmed flowers and foliage to conceal the foam and provide visual depth. Finally, put the spray on the floor to check that the foliage and smaller flowers appear to radiate from the main flowers. If there are any gaps, fill in with a flower or piece of foliage, then lightly spray with water before storing.

WHAT YOU WILL NEED

Plastic tray filled with wet foam, pot tape, foliage, such as Tsuga pine, *Abies grandis* or cupressus, bold flowers for the focal point, and filler flowers.

1 *Sharpen the foliage ends with a knife and insert them securely in the foam, placing them low down and creating a pear shape. The handle of the base is at the rounded end of the foliage outline.*

2 *The graded bold flowers are now placed on different levels to form a focal point line in the centre of the tribute. The main flower is placed two-thirds of the way down the design, and is single-leg mounted.*

3 *To fill in the design, start at the foliage outline and insert flowers on different levels and in diagonal lines, remembering that all materials must appear to radiate from the focal flower.*

Here are the different types of funeral spray. The smaller, natural design is the single-ended spray, and the larger and more impressive tribute is the double-ended spray.

CREMATION OR SYMPATHY BASKET

A well-made basket of lovely flowers and foliage is an appropriate tribute, particularly if it is to be sent to a hospital or nursing home, in memory of the deceased. A basket of this type provides an attractive decoration, easy to look after and with good lasting qualities.

Method of assembly

Select a basket with a solid base and a tall strong handle; the basket must be watertight – either lined or with a liner added. Take a third, half or whole brick of wet foam, depending on the size of the basket, and place it in the centre, allowing 2.5cm (1in) of foam to project above the rim. Secure the foam by passing coated wire through the centre of the foam and twisting the ends around the base of the handle. If you have any available, pack damp moss around the sides of the foam for added security.

Insert pieces of foliage horizontally, establishing the length and width of the design and forming a diamond shape. Using stems of bud flowers, strengthen the outline, then add focal point flowers in a gently curved diagonal line, remembering to leave plenty of space for the handle. Fill in with materials on all levels, to give an elevated profile, and recess short-stemmed flowers and pieces of foliage to hide the foam. Now spray lightly and store in the cool room until delivered.

Fill the basket with wet foam, firmly attached with wire. Insert the foliage, creating a basic diamond. Strengthen the outline by adding flowers on various levels, ensuring that materials do not interfere with the handle. To finish the basket, insert the main flowers and recess some materials. Add the card, and the basket is ready for delivery.

WHAT YOU WILL NEED

Foliage types (including Tsuga pine, eucalyptus, *Viburnum davidii* and leatherleaf), flowers (tulips, freesias, alstroemeria, carnation spray, hyacinths and small roses), damp moss, if available, a third of a brick of wet foam, and a strong basket with a firm handle.

Remember that the design will be viewed from all sides, and materials should be kept low, so they do not interfere with the handle.

AN OPEN POSY

When ordering flowers for a funeral, many customers prefer to send a natural-looking tribute, such as an open posy or basket. The open posy can be made in a range of sizes, and various combinations of flowers and foliage can be used. This would be a suitable tribute to suggest for a child's funeral or for a design to be sent on behalf of children to the funeral of a grandparent, aunt, uncle, cousin or friend.

Preparing the posy

With the materials and container ready and prepared, start by using a sharp knife to cut foliage stems to points, then insert the foliage securely into the foam to form a circular outline around the rim of the container.

Add pieces of foliage to the top of the foam to create a domed profile. Next, add a curving line of focal flowers, the main flower being the tallest, and positioned at the centre. Fill in the outline shape with the bud materials. Insert open flowers and pieces of foliage at varying levels to fill in the centre of the design and to strengthen the elevated profile.

Recess some flowers and foliage to hide the foam and give visual depth. Look at the posy from all angles to check that it is complete and that no foam has been left visible. Spray lightly and store in the chiller.

WHAT YOU WILL NEED

Foliage types, which can include Tsuga pine, leatherleaf, cupressus, asparagus tops, trails of hedera, and hebe; flowers, which can include alstroemeria, carnation spray, roses, sweet peas, cornflowers, scabious, anemones, double tulips, and chrysanthemum spray; plastic container, cylinder of wet foam, and pot tape.

This informal tribute can be made with a variety of flowers and foliage types.

SHEAVES

Flower arrangements have become increasingly informal in recent years, and this also applies to sympathy flowers. Formal tributes remain popular in some areas, but many people now prefer to see informal arrangements, such as sheaves, which, because they are not wrapped, have an immediate impact.

These can vary enormously in appearance according to the selection of flowers, and they also range a great deal in price. In springtime, a sheaf might be very economically made with daffodils, tulips and irises, but the same design, made as a very special tribute and containing red roses and choice foliage, would be correspondingly expensive.

Construction

The spiralling of the stems is vital to the construction, giving the design profile. All stems running from left to right are placed on top of the main stem, and those running from right to left are added behind it; in this way, the spiral is built up.

The design must have a flat back so that it does not rock when laid down, and the best way to achieve this is to use a strong flat piece of foliage, such as *Abies grandis*. To complete the sheaf, it must be firmly tied, and a large bow of an appropriate colour added. The stems are then trimmed to shape, roughly one-third of the length of the design.

WHAT YOU WILL NEED

***Abies grandis*, gerberas, liatris, alstroemeria, tulips, twine and ribbon.**

1 *The materials are prepared. The* Abies grandis *is set out in a fan shape, and the leaves have been cleaned off the lower half of the stems.*

2 *The outline is formed with the longer-stemmed materials, and the profile is built up by spiralling the stems.*

The richness of the yellow
and purple sheaf is
enhanced by the glossy
purple ribbon.

A CHAPLET

A chaplet is a design often requested for men and women who have served in the forces, and immediately brings to mind images of military memorial services. In Greek and Roman times, the laurel chaplet was not only used at funerals but was also presented in the same way that we would now award a medal for outstanding performance. A victorious hero would wear wreaths around his neck, and the chaplet would be placed on his head. Even today, a foliage chaplet or wreath is still given to the winner of a motor race.

The base of a chaplet can be massed in flowers or foliage, and the cluster can either be placed opposite the point or to one side, asymmetrically.

Laurel chaplets

If laurel, *Prunus laurocerasus*, is to be used, as here, the leaves must be a good shape, and free from insect damage or disease. Grading the leaves into different sizes will help you to emphasize the tailored shape of the design.

Laurel leaves can be utilized in a variety of ways. Three methods are used in this design: some leaves are used flat and loop stitched (see page 145) for support and control; others are curled at the base to give a pointed appearance and then pinned to the base of the chaplet, and some are rolled onto themselves and pins are placed inside the curl, attaching the leaves to the base. Each of these methods can either be employed singly or in combination.

Finishing touches

When the foliage basing is complete, give the leaves a coating of leaf shine for a lovely glossy finish. Other foliage can be used in this type of design – the golden-leaved and the silver-leaved varieties of eleagnus are effective, as are camellia leaves and the larger varieties of hedera.

The foliage base requires a bold cluster of flowers to complement it. The exotic foliage of Joseph's coat, *Codiaeum pictum*, harmonizes with the gerberas and the lime-green Singapore orchids to give an exotic feel to the cluster on the chaplet.

WHAT YOU WILL NEED

A mossed chaplet frame, a quantity of laurel, mini-gerberas, Singapore orchids, alstroemeria buds, codiaeum foliage, ivy berries, and eucalyptus foliage.

1 *Laurel leaves are loop stitched and are inserted firmly into the moss frame, radiating outwards from the proposed cluster point.*

2 *The foam for the cluster is attached to the frame. Curled laurel leaves are graded in size, and pinned on the frame with German pins.*

3 *Rolled laurel leaves complete the foliage base. Eucalyptus foliage is inserted into the plastic foam to provide the outline to the cluster.*

The red mini-gerberas stand out boldly against the green, glossy foliage of the tailored base.

BASING FORMAL TRIBUTES

A formal tribute is the name given to a design in which the base is completely covered with flowers, foliage or mosses, and is finished with sprays or clusters. Several different terms are used to describe this covering technique, including massing, blocking, bedding and – the term we have chosen to use here – basing.

The skill of basing is to bond the materials together to give an even and uniform base while making sure that you retain the distinctive shape – a heart, cross, pillow or chaplet – of the tribute.

For moss foundations, small, medium and large flowers are double-leg mounted, the wire being inserted through the base of the flower. For a plastic foam frame, simply cut flowers into three groups.

Materials for basing

It is important to select materials which will bond together and give maximum coverage, with no visible gaps. Basing should create a bevelled effect, with the chosen materials starting at the ribbon or foliage edge and gradually building up onto and covering the top of the frame, finishing by the foam bump.

Flowers used for basing include chrysanthemum sprays, carnations, open roses and daffodils, and wired clusters of flowers such as violets, stocks, narcissi, Sweet Williams and hydrangeas. Suitable foliage includes laurel, hedera, camellia and eucalyptus. Bun moss must, if used, be green and fresh.

Using spray chrysanthemums

Grade the flowers into three groups – small, medium and large – leaving stems of 3.75cm (1½in) on smaller flowers, and 5-8cm (2-3in) on larger ones.

Insert bud flowers to establish a clear outline; use medium flowers to build up the bevelled effect, and fill in the top of the frame with large flowers. Finally, fill in any gaps with small buds, and complete the tribute by adding a spray or cluster.

WHAT YOU WILL NEED

Plastic foam frame or mossed and backed frame, fans of cupressus or pleated ribbon, German pins or glue gun, and flowers for basing.

For a mossed frame, the small flowers are inserted first, to establish the inner and outer rings; the medium flowers then form the next ring, and the large flowers the centre one. All rings must bond together in a bevelled effect.

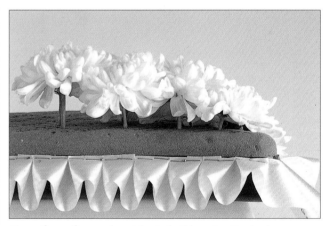

For a foam frame, box-pleated ribbon is attached as an edging. Insert an outline row of bud flowers just above the ribbon; add a second row of medium flowers at a 45 degree angle, to establish the bevelling effect.

To complete the plastic foam frame, add lines of large open flowers vertically, filling in the centre of the design up to the foam bump. Finish with a spray or cluster.

A FORMAL POSY

A design that has become popular in recent years, the formal posy is also called a posy pad. Dainty and pretty, it is a suitable tribute to be sent either to older relatives from children or to a child.

The ribbon edging is straightforward to attach with the German pins, although a little extra care is required to ensure a neat finish at the join. It is as well not to draw attention to the join by putting it at the 'front'; instead, it can be placed either to one side or at the rear of the cluster.

The chrysanthemums are cut with sufficiently long stems to allow them to be inserted firmly into the foam base. Chrysanthemums at the outer edge can be wired (see pages 50-53) for extra security. The outer ring of flowers must not obscure the ribbon edging. The basing must be even and have a smooth finish, with flowers bevelled towards the cluster to give the whole base a rounded profile.

The cluster

The cluster generally has a definite outline – for example, round, diamond, crescent or, as in the pictured design, a teardrop. Foliage creates the initial outline of the cluster. Pernettya shrub, eucalyptus, and the larger leaves of *Hedera canariensis* are used to give depth and unity.

The roses, as focal flowers, define the profile. Carnation sprays are added to strengthen the focal flowers and provide further texture. Lily buds offer a contrast both in form and in texture, and a strong grouping of muscari and individual hyacinth pips, together with the finishing touch of a ribbon bow, help to complete the cluster.

This design features a single placement of flowers, but secondary placements can also be effective, especially if linked to the principal placement by foliage or ribbon.

WHAT YOU WILL NEED

Posy pad, ribbon, double chrysanthemum spray, roses, carnation spray, muscari, hyacinths, lily buds, and a selection of dainty types of foliage.

1 *Box-pleated ribbon is used for the edging of this posy pad. The double white chrysanthemums are added in neat rows, bevelled towards the cluster to give a rounded profile.*

2 *The chrysanthemum base is completed – it is neat and has a smooth finish. Hedera is added to establish the outline of the cluster, which is in the shape of a teardrop.*

The formal posy is a design often requested for elderly relatives on behalf of children. This lovely tribute, with its combination of soft peach 'Gerdo' roses and blue muscari and hyacinths, might be given to a grandfather by his grandson.

A BASED HEART

One of the favourite funeral tributes is a heart, representing love and affection, especially from a close member of the family. It is often requested as a sympathy tribute from a husband or wife. The design shown here might be made in different shades of pink if it were for a woman, perhaps from her husband, and carnations might replace the single crysanthemum.

It is not usually necessary to wire the flowers going into the foam, but sometimes, if the stems are a little soft, it is advisable to wire the few that form the point, for extra security. The ribbon edging is box pleated, and can be secured to the frame either with German pins or with a glue gun.

The foam bump must be firmly screwed into the base before the spray is made. The outline materials and main flowers can be support wired if necessary. The spray should tone in with the base flowers. The spray is diamond-shaped, and should be a third the size of the completed design. The central rose is the highest in the spray, with the other flowers used to build the profile.

WHAT YOU WILL NEED

Foam heart frame, ribbon, German pins, stapler, foam bump, 0.71mm (22 gauge) green annealed wires, chrysanthemums for basing, and flowers for spray.

---

1 *The foam is trimmed and soaked before the ribbon edging is attached with German pins. To give a good outline shape, start basing around the edge.*

2 *Add the foam bump, and continue to fill in the design, using single chrysanthemum flowers.*

3 *The outline of the spray is formed, and the main line of the roses is added.*

A beautiful heart, based in pink single chrysanthe-mums, is offset by a spray of 'Jacaranda' roses and choice foliage.

GIFT WRAPPING

Gift wrapping is the term that describes the packing materials and techniques used by the florist to pack cut flowers, handtied designs, arrangements and gifts attractively. It is the first impression of a gift that always lingers in the memory of the recipient. Imagine receiving a gift in plain wrapping paper – the gift inside might be fantastic, but the boring packaging would not arouse the same excitement that you would feel if the gift had been beautifully wrapped and trimmed to match.

The florist not only sells a wide variety of lovely products, but also offers a unique gift-wrapping service, using a range of boxes, cylinders, cellophanes and beautiful ribbons, all of which, when used with skill and imagination, enhance the appearance and increase the impact of gifts.

USES OF GIFT WRAPPING

No amount of cellophane or ribbon can improve the beauty of a perfect single rose or an armful of summer flowers. But gift wrapping does have many advantages.

The clever use of ribbons can enhance the colour of the flowers or give an appropriate sense of occasion. Cellophane protects delicate flower heads and makes handling easier. Covered flowers and foliage are also protected from rapid changes in weather or temperature, which can have a detrimental effect on the cut materials.

Water can be added to the stem ends enclosed in cellophane to give them a temporary resevoir, thus delaying water loss and wilting. Using this method, flowers can be gift-wrapped well in advance.

Simple posy
This dainty all-round posy of lemon roses and cream chrysanthemums is simply wrapped in cellophane and decorated with a matching yellow ribbon.

Wrapped bouquet
The rich purple ribbon accentuates the colour of the freesias contained within this cellophane gift wrap.

Tied design
This handtied design
allows the beauty of
the summer flowers
to be immediately enjoyed.
The decorative ribbon
repeats the textures
and colours of the
bouquet.

Cylinder
A cylinder is the perfect receptacle for these
beautiful flowers, as it protects them from
being crushed. The stem ends are kept in a
small test tube of water to prevent them
dehydrating.

Box pack
The cellophane
box pack protects these
Harvest Moon carnations while
allowing their beauty to be enjoyed.
The ribbon matches perfectly the soft golden
colour of the flowers.

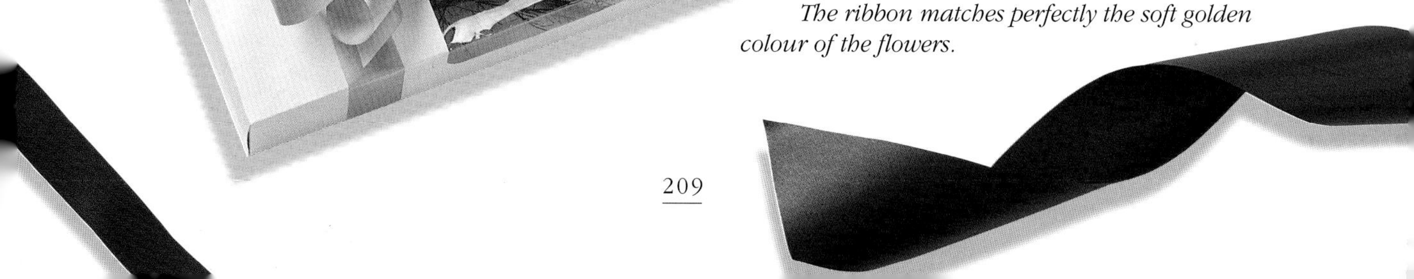

GIFT-WRAPPED CUT FLOWERS

A lovely selection of flowers, with carefully chosen foliage, professionally arranged in cellophane and trimmed with an attractive ribbon bow, is a gift suitable for many occasions, including birthdays or anniversaries, and makes a charming way of saying 'Get well soon' or 'Thank you'.

WHAT YOU WILL NEED

Roll of cellophane or cellocoup, ribbon to blend with the flowers, tying twine or tape, stapler and staples, packet of flower food, care card, greetings card in envelope, selection of cut flowers as ordered (with long and short stems, and including some special flowers), and foliage.

1 *Cut a length of cellophane. Place long-stemmed materials first, adding flowers to the right and left, special flowers in the centre, and then short-stemmed flowers at the bottom. Tie stems firmly together.*

Almost any type of flower can be gift wrapped. Rolls of cellophane can be fitted on a rack with serrated edges for easy cutting, and you can then take lengths as required. The latest range includes cellophanes decorated with hearts, flowers, stars or company names, as well as coloured types, which can be coordinated with the flowers.

Method

Collect together all equipment, flowers and foliage, and check that the bench is clean. Make a bow with streamers, then cut a length of cellophane, twice as long as the flowers and foliage, plus 30cm (12in). Lay the cellophane on your workbench, then place the long-stemmed materials and stems of foliage on the lower half of the cellophane. Add flowers to the right and left, then place special flowers in the centre, grouping them in lines.

Add short-stemmed materials near the bottom, ensuring that all flowers are displayed to their best advantage and will not be crushed. Tie all stems securely together, and remove any foliage beneath the tying point. Bring the cellophane over the flowers, making sure that stems are covered.

At the sides, fold under 2.5cm (1in) of cellophane, forming a neat edge, and staple at intervals. Gather the cellophane at the tying point and firmly secure a bow over it. Finally, attach a packet of flower food, together with a care card and envelope.

2 *Carefully centre the bouquet on the lower half of the cellophane; cover the flowers with the other half, ensuring that stems are well protected.*

3 *At each side, fold under 2.5cm (1in) of cellophane. Staple evenly along each side, gathering at the tying point to avoid crushing and to permit air circulation.*

A selection of beautiful flowers and foliage, gift wrapped, is a popular and well-received gift.

A MODERN HANDTIED DESIGN

For many years, assistants in flower shops in Europe have held flowers in the hand as the customer chose them, and then tied them together with twine, to produce a carefully organized bunch, ready to be placed straight in a vase.

The design shown here is very modern in shape, and demands flowers that have a great deal of impact, plus inbuilt space, to show them off. Gerberas are ideal for this purpose, but must sometimes be support wired, allowing the stems to be bent without damage. Liatris, with their strong straight stems, are excellent for providing height. Large leaves look good, but again it is advisable to wire them so that they can be positioned horizontally. Bear grass softens the outline of this design.

WHAT YOU WILL NEED

A selection of dramatic flowers, such as gerberas, and other materials to give height and width, 0.71mm (22 gauge) green annealed wires, twine, cellophane, and matching ribbon.

2 The height is achieved by using purple liatris, and width is provided by a combination of fatsia leaves, golden gerberas and bear grass.

1 The gerberas are support wired with 0.71mm (22 gauge) green annealed wires before being tied into the bunch with green twine.

3 The tied bunch is wrapped with clear cellophane for protection and impact. A golden ribbon bow adds the finishing touch.

This dramatic design of golden gerberas and purple liatris is perfect for a modern room.

WRAPPING ARRANGEMENTS

Arrangements benefit from being gift wrapped, as this protects them from extremes of temperature and helps to preserve an atmosphere of high humidity, so that flowers arrive at their destination at the peak of perfection. In addition, the perceived value of a gift-wrapped arrangement is greater than the actual outlay for sundries, and this is good, both for the florist and for the purchaser.

There are many ways of gift wrapping, or 'gifting', flower designs, and the simple method shown here uses a good quality cellophane, with ample thickness to enable it to stand by itself.

Cut a generous amount of cellophane, and bring the ends up to join at the top of the arrangement. Scrunch them together, and fasten with cellotape. The open sides of the cellophane are brought together and joined with cellotape.

Underneath the arrangement, the cellophane can be pleated around the container where necessary, and again fixed with cellotape, to make handling easier.

The design is completed with a harmonizing ribbon bow.

2 *The cellophane is joined over the top of the arrangement with cellotape; here, the sides remain open and have yet to be joined.*

1 *Gather together the items required for the gift wrapping – the arrangement, the cellophane (plain or patterned), ribbon and cellotape.*

3 *The cellophane gift wrapping is completed. A ribbon bow is made in an appropriate colour, ready to be attached to the design.*

This beautiful all-round design looks even more appealing with the addition of the gift wrapping, yet the flowers are easily seen.

BOXES OF FLOWERS

An elegant box of flowers and foliage is a glamorous gift and makes an attractive alternative to a bouquet in cellophane. Boxes are available in different styles and sizes, ranging from a big box, capable of holding a large quantity of flowers, to the specially-designed slim box, containing a water bottle to hold a single rose for Valentine's Day or a similar romantic occasion. The range includes white, coloured, patterned and printed boxes, with or without cellophane windows, and there are two basic designs – a one-piece folded box, with attached lid and special liner, and a two-piece folded box with separate lid. Assembly is fiddly, but can be mastered with practice.

WHAT YOU WILL NEED

A selection of flowers and foliage with long, medium and short stems, a box pack, lining materials, tying twine or tape, ribbon to blend with the flowers, flower food, care card, and greetings card.

Advantages

Boxes are delivered as flat packs, so are easy to store, and at peak sales times ready-packed boxes of flowers can be stacked in delivery areas and then quickly packed into the van. (Remember to place the envelope where it can easily be seen.) A box also gives protection against severe weather, is easy to carry, and prevents the flowers from being crushed.

Assembling a box pack

Collect all materials, equipment, flowers, and foliage. Working on a clean bench, make up the box, inserting a white or colour coordinated paper lining if none is supplied. Place long-stemmed materials in the box first; fill in the sides, and place special flowers at the centre. Finish with short-stemmed flowers at the bottom. Tie the stems firmly together, perhaps adding a bow to cover this. Place flower food and a care card inside; secure the lid with cellotape, and finish with the greetings card, and a ribbon trim, if desired.

1 Select and assemble a box of the correct size for the length of the flowers, following the manufacturer's instructions, and taking care not to damage it. Add lining paper, and then practise assembling the flowers beside the box.

2 Insert the long-stemmed flowers and foliage, then add flowers of medium length, filling in the sides and centre.

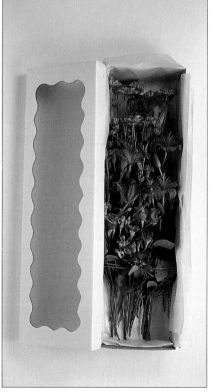

3 Integrate short-stemmed flowers near the tying point. Gather and tie securely – a ribbon bow can be added.

A large box can hold a
lavish selection of flowers,
while a slim, elegant box
is for the romantically
inclined.

CYLINDERS OR TUBES

A single rose is the classic token of love and affection, but to wrap it in shop paper would detract from its initial romantic impact. To enhance the flower, we need to add complementary packaging.

Single flowers in cylinders or tubes are suitable for most occasions. They are especially popular on Valentine's Day, when a single red rose with a piece of asparagus fern is placed in the tube and decorated with red ribbon, but they are also appropriate for Christmas, birthdays and anniversaries. Although roses are normally used in cylinders, there is no reason why other flowers, such as spray carnations, freesias or orchids should not be given in tubes of this type.

Cylinders

In the picture, an acetate cylinder has been used. Such containers come in many shapes and sizes, and are available from most florist's wholesalers or from specialized packaging companies.

To keep it fresh, the flower stem is placed either in a small tube containing water and cut flower food or in a piece of wet foam.

Decorating

There is no correct or incorrect way to decorate an acetate container. It is a matter of taste, and also of your customer's particular likes and dislikes. Do not forget that he or she is the one paying for the design.

When choosing a ribbon to decorate your cylinder, remember that there are now many that are specially designed for occasions such as Valentine's Day or Christmas. Featured here is one decorated with small red hearts. This ribbon makes preformed bows if you pull a cord.

The cylinders in the picture are simply enhanced by taking the ribbon around the tube and attaching it with cellotape at the top and bottom. They are completed with a well-made bow of special ribbon, attached to the lid.

WHAT YOU WILL NEED

An acetate cylinder (here, with wet foam), a single rose, a piece of asparagus fern, ribbon to decorate, and cellotape.

1 The stem of the rose and a piece of fern are placed into the wet foam and both are gently eased into the tube. The ribbon bow for the top is prepared.

2 Ribbon is attached to the top and bottom of the cylinder with cellotape, and ribbon is wound around the bottom of the cylinder to conceal the foam.

A cylinder with a rose is a delightful gift for Valentine's Day, or maybe for a birthday.

THE FLORIST'S YEAR

The florist's year is busy but productive. The hours are often long and arduous, but the pleasures are many.
A glittering arrangement, complete with champagne, balloons and novelty hats, ushers in the New Year. Special events around the year give many reasons to celebrate with romantic red roses for Valentine's Day, pretty posies and handtied bunches for Mother's Day, and then the joyful abundance of Easter flowers after Lenten austerities.

Christmas, with its traditional holly, mistletoe, pine, spruce, ivy, candles and glitter, plus a whole host of other possibilities for the more adventurous, is the peak of the florist's year. In between these events is a constant stream of weddings, large and small, christenings, birthdays and special anniversaries toasted with champagne.

The hours may be long and the work strenuous, but the look of pleasure on the face of a bride or a new mum, makes all the effort worthwhile.

CELEBRATE WITH FLOWERS

Throughout the year, the florist is a key element in the round of celebrations – seasonal, national, religious or traditional, plus a host of personal anniversaries and events. Each country has its own days of national significance – Anzac Day in Australia, Thanksgiving and Independence Day in the United States, St George's Day in England, St David's Day in Wales, St Andrew's Day in Scotland, and, of course, St Patrick's Day, celebrated by the Irish the world over. In each case, either flowers in the national colours or specific flowers – red rose buttonholes in England, daffodils in Wales, Irish shamrocks – will be requested. The florist must be prepared for all these seasonal demands, and for the personal preferences and requirements of individual customers – delicate flowers for a new baby, silvers and golds for wedding anniversaries, and red roses for lovers.

The seasons

In every country, the seasons bring their own particular delights, but the florist is also aware of the multi-cultural and international associations with different seasons and can therefore satisfy, with a host of imported, 'early' or 'late' materials, the requests of each and every customer.

Spring

When spring arrives, daffodils, tulips, hyacinths and many other spring flowers have already been available for some months, but this is the season we associate with these flowers. Bright, cheerful colours in natural baskets are tempting.

Early summer

Lilies of the valley, peonies, broom, cow parsley and achillea are just a few of the lovely summer flowers that we can expect to see now.

Summer

Foxgloves, sweet peas, roses, snapdragons, lilies and liatris are among the flowers that are associated with this time of year. Cool blues and white are appealing during summer, when the weather is hot and sultry.

Autumn

Russets, warm reds and oranges are the colours that we associate with the cooler temperatures of autumn, chrysanthemums, dahlias, asters and nerines being among the seasonal flowers.

Winter

Snowdrops, winter-flowering jasmine and viburnums are associated with this bleak time of year, along with evergreens.

Christmas

Christmas designs can be requested throughout the Advent period and up to Christmas Eve.

Designs Door wreaths, gift arrangements, memorial designs, and decorated Christmas trees.

Colours Reds, greens and blue-greens are traditional, but pinks and silvers, and blues and silvers, are also in demand.

Flowers The Christmas rose (*Helleborus niger*), the poinsettia and, of course, holly, ivy and mistletoe evoke the seasonal cheer, but carnations, chrysanthemums, narcissi, hyacinths and other flowers are used in gift arrangements.

Accessories Candles, cones, fruits, nuts, baubles, little Santas, parcels, Christmas tree decorations, and all sorts of novelty items can be utilized in arrangements for gifts and the home.

Easter

The date varies, but Easter is always in late March or during April.

Designs Church arrangements for the altar

and window sills, and large designs for the chancel steps; for the home, arrangements can be made in baskets and pottery.

Colours Yellow and white

Flowers Arum and longiflorum lilies, along with daffodils and narcissi; the abundance of flowers in church is lovely after the abstinence of Lent; for home decoration, spring flowers are favoured.

Accessories Fluffy little chicks, nests and Easter eggs.

Father's Day

Designs Gift arrangements in rough pottery containers.

Colours Strong masculine colours.

Flowers Bold materials, such as gerberas or chrysanthemums, and perhaps the tropical flowers, such as banksia and gingers.

Accessories Gifts for Dad can vary from a gardening tool to football socks.

Hallowe'en

Designs Party arrangements.

Colours Reds, oranges and blacks.

Flowers Those with unusual or insect-like forms, such as spider chrysanthemums or pincushion proteas.

Accessories Pumpkins, witches' hats, spiders and cobwebs; dried materials can help to give a spooky feel to designs.

Jewish New Year

This is a movable date, but always in September.

Designs Gift arrangements, baskets and plant designs.

Colours Cheerful and bright, although there are no special colours.

Flowers Seasonal flowers and the more expensive choice flowers are all welcomed as gifts at this happy time.

Mother's Day

Designs Posies, baskets and dainty gift arrangements.

Colours Pinks, lemons and most pastels.

Flowers Traditionally, customers opt for small dainty flowers, such as primulas and narcissi, as well as carnations and roses; pussy willow and catkins are also appealing.

Accessories Gift wrapping and pretty ribbon bows to harmonize with the flowers.

National Memorial Days

Designs Memorial tributes, such as chaplets and wreaths.

Colours Reds and greens are usually asked for, but regimental, battalion or flight colours may be requested.

Flowers Red poppies, in memory of the red poppies covering the Flanders fields after World War 1; carnations and roses are also popular. Another idea would be to include rosemary for remembrance.

Accessories Ribbons in the colours of the regiment.

New Year's Day

Designs Party arrangements for homes and hotels.

Colours Bright and exciting.

Flowers No particularly appropriate flowers, but choose bold forms from among your cut materials.

Accessories Ribbon streamers, party poppers and balloons.

Thanksgiving and Harvest Festival

Designs Church window sills and special free-standing arrangements.

Colours Orange, red-orange and yellows.

Flowers Chrysanthemums, dahlias, and other seasonal flowers; wheat ears, barley and other grains are often used in designs.

Accessories Fruits and vegetables are an obvious choice, and farm tools, such as scythes, are used to represent the harvesting of crops in these interpretive designs.

Valentine's Day

Designs Single flowers, bouquets, handtied flowers, and arrangements of all possible descriptions.

Colours Reds, scarlets and pinks.

Flowers Roses, carnations; red flowers are always scarce, so use other bold and bright colours to make exciting designs.

Accessories Extravagant gift wrapping, with lots of hearts and arrows.

A GREETINGS CARD

The greetings card arrangement is a novelty design with great appeal to people of all ages, and it is particularly appropriate for those occasions when a card is normally sent – a birthday or anniversary, or when congratulations are due for some special achievement.

Unlike some novelty containers, a card is easy for the arranger. The design may be a loose triangular shape or asymmetrical. The flowers selected are generally choice varieties, as there is a limit to the size of design that can be made. Suitable flowers include Singapore orchids, spray roses, bridal gladioli, muscari, and double-flowered tulips.

WHAT YOU WILL NEED

Greetings card container, small plastic dish, cylinder of foam, pot tape or glue gun, five roses, four stems of carnation spray and two of chrysanthemum, a bunch of freesias, a ribbon bow, and a selection of foliage types.

To assemble the design

Gather together the card and all other materials. Prepare the mechanics by soaking the foam cylinder and putting it into the container. The card has a back section to hold the container and to allow customers to water their design, but for added security, attach the foam and container to the card with pot tape. Alternatively, the container can be fixed to the card with a glue gun or pot.

The flowers and foliage can now be added to the container. For height, a dainty spray of carnations is inserted so that it reaches above the top level of the card. More materials are added at the sides of the card, the openings being used to extend the design beyond the card.

The roses – the focal flowers – are taken down the centre of the card, the finest rose being used for the focal point.

Freesias and other materials are added so that they all appear to flow from behind the focal point. There is little filling-in to do, as the card itself hides the mechanics.

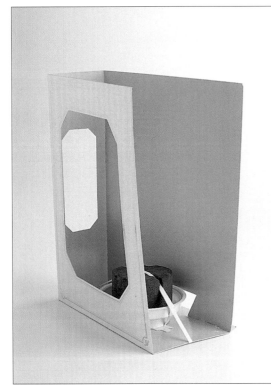

1 *The mechanics for the greetings card are prepared. The side opening, which allows the flowers to be arranged so that they flow out at both sides, can clearly be seen.*

2 *The outline materials are added in a loose triangular shape.* Nephrolepis *and* Skimmia japonica *foliage is placed towards the centre of the design, to provide visual weight.*

These warm and glowing colours would be a joy to receive on a special day – the card simply overflows with exquisite flowers.

FLOWER GIFTS

F lowers are a wonderful gift for any occasion, and can express love, sorrow, joy and happiness. Floral gifts come in all shapes and sizes, including arrangements, cards and handtieds. Cellophane, ribbon and accessories can be used to enhance a gift of flowers, and turn it into something personal.

Anniversaries

Whether the occasion is a wedding anniversary or a birthday, an arrangement always makes a popular gift, as the recipient has no work to do. A ribbon bow or bows in an appropriate colour can be added – red for a ruby wedding gift, silver for a 25th or gold for a 50th. Keys are used for 18th or 21st birthday arrangements. Handtied bunches, wrapped in cellophane, are also excellent, as they are ready to be placed directly in a vase, after recutting the stems.

Births

The range of containers includes lace cradles, pottery and basketware. Pinks and whites are usual for girls; blues, yellow and cream for boys. Again, there are many delightful accessories that might be added.

A 21st birthday present
Something bright and cheerful to celebrate a 21st birthday – the lovely ceramic pot displays the 'Eoliet' gerberas to perfection.

Congratulations!
For a day to remember, this stunning arrangement of 'Eurovision' lilies, freesias, and 'Belinda' roses will capture that glowing feeling.

Lace cradle

Traditional, but still exquisite, this lace cradle overflows with dainty flowers and foliage; wooden alphabet blocks complete the design.

Something for father

Any father would appreciate this attractive pewter tankard, with its strong, bold arrangement of veronica, gerberas and bluebells.

House warming present

This attractive and practical gift contains glowing peach and gold flowers, arranged in two cast-iron saucepans.

ANNIVERSARY ARRANGEMENTS

O ver many years, wedding anniversaries have been given names that indicate the most suitable gift for the occasion. There are several variations on the lesser anniversaries, and it is as well to keep a list of the traditional names and the more modern equivalents.

Flowers have their own special anniversary – the fourth year – but they are an acceptable gift for all anniversaries. Try to ensure that the flowers or accessories reflect the theme of the anniversary. With the landmark anniversaries – silver, ruby and gold – colour is important, and there are many accessories available to help emphasize a particular idea.

Larkspur, phlox, and lilies make a summery selection of flowers to celebrate 25 years of marriage; perhaps this bride carried a bouquet of summer blooms all those years ago.

Silver wedding anniversary

A family get-together or a party will often accompany this anniversary, to help the couple celebrate their 25 years of marriage. Arrangements for the home or for the party should continue to reflect the silver theme. Flowers in pinks, pale lilac and white are put together with silver ribbons, little silver picks and, more recently, silver congratulation balloons.

Customers often bring silver bowls or vases to be filled with flowers for the occasion. To protect the container and to enable the flower preservatives to work effectively, use a liner or inner plastic container.

The arrangement pictured here is a delicious combination of flowers and foliage types. Larkspur, veronica, phlox, lilies, freesias, anemones and carnations make a lovely summer bouquet for an anniversary couple.

Golden wedding anniversary

There is something very special about those couples who have been married for 50 years. Over the next decade, florists will see couples who were married during, or just after, the war years, when flowers and fabrics for wedding dresses were scarce.

These couples will now be in their seventies, and the mellow golds, bronzes and oranges of the flowers in this golden wedding anniversary design are an apt colour harmony for fifty years of marriage. Softly-coloured gerberas blend with roses, lilies, chrysanthemums and carnations in this upright basket. The addition of a greetings card would complete the picture.

To customers ordering flowers, suggest designs that are easy to look after or require little or no arranging, unless, of course, one of the recipients is a flower arranger.

With other wedding anniversaries, choose a container, accessory or, perhaps, a colour combination that reflects the nature of the anniversary. The first, or cotton anniversary, could include natural stems of cotton-wool seed heads; for the twentieth, you might have dainty flowers in a china vase.

Right *The rich gold and bronze colourings include 'Golden Times', the perfect name for a rose that is to be included in a golden wedding anniversary arrangement.*

MOTHER'S DAY

This is one of the most important, and busiest, occasions in the florist's calendar. At Christmas, customers accept that arrangements will be sent out throughout the week preceding the event, but Mother's Day arrangements must go out on the Saturday and Sunday, resulting in long working hours for florists and their drivers.

Mother's Day has evolved from the time when many people were in service and away from home. On just one day a year they were allowed to visit their families, the fourth Sunday in Lent being chosen because it marked the end of fasting, so families could celebrate and feast together.

Flowers are sold in many styles for Mother's Day, from gift-wrapped bunches for mothers who enjoy arranging their own flowers, to handtied bunches, ready to be placed in a vase.

Posy pad

A posy pad base is ideal for this occasion, for it enables flowers and a gift to be incorporated into one design. The ribbon seen here is box pleated and stapled; it is attached to the frame with a cool melt gun – a hot gun might damage the ribbon.

The base is held under the tap for a minute or two to soak the foam.

Flowers and foliage are added at different heights to create interest, and it is important to include an attractive variety both of textures and of shapes. This type of design is also ideal for birthdays and other anniversaries and for Christmas.

The flowers may be given a fine misting before the gift is added, but once the gift is in place, make sure that it does not get wet. A piece of cellophane is placed under the gift to keep it dry.

WHAT YOU WILL NEED

A posy pad, ribbon, stapler, glue gun, 'Gerdo' roses, spray carnations, freesias, and a good selection of foliage types.

1 *The edge of the posy pad is trimmed, and a pleated ribbon is glued in place. The 'Gerdo' roses are a perfect match with the peach-coloured ribbon.*

2 *The design is built up with peach and cream flowers and a selection of beautiful foliage types, set on different levels to give interest and depth to the arrangement.*

A charming gift is set in a dainty arrangement of roses and freesias.

MOTHER'S DAY DESIGNS

Flowers are the favourite gift for Mother's Day, and every year the public spend thousands of pounds on flowers to celebrate this special occasion.

Preparations for Mother's Day include the following:

● Keep lists of previous years' sales to assist with the ordering.
● Make out delivery routes and check that the drivers know the areas.
● Write out all cards well in advance.
● Make sure that all staff, and temporary staff in particular, understand the shop procedures.
● Set up containers and green the week before.

Over the years, the preference for certain designs has changed, from the bunches of primroses and violets of the early years of this century, through to formal rigid arrangements in the 1960s and 1970s and back to handtied informal designs for the 1990s.

The choice of flowers has also changed dramatically, probably because these days nearly every variety is available all year round. As well as the usual carnations, spray carnations, roses, freesias, and flowers such as muscari, double and single tulips, hyacinths and daffodils, it is possible to buy larkspur, lilac, lilies and also exotics, such as anthuriums, ginger and orchids.

Mothers love flowers; they love them in any shape, size and colour. Florists' shops are therefore able to send out a huge variety of arrangements, as well as bunches of cut flowers and handtied designs. Included in these would be posy bowls, traditional symmetrical and asymmetrical arrangements, modern and European designs, cards, posy pads, baskets, planted bowls and pots-et-fleurs.

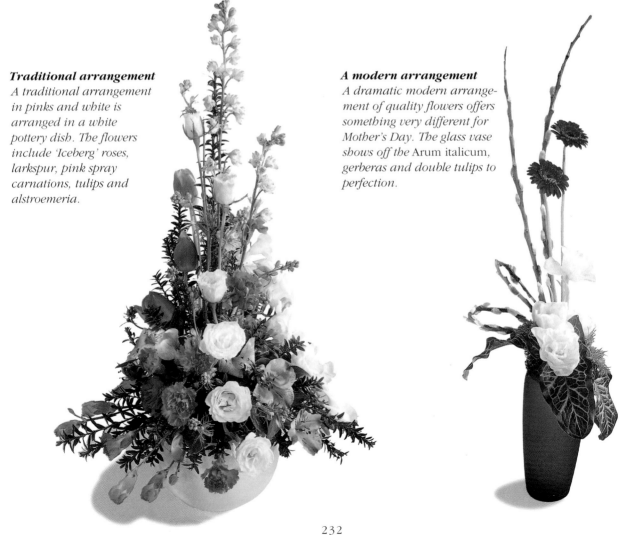

Traditional arrangement
A traditional arrangement in pinks and white is arranged in a white pottery dish. The flowers include 'Iceberg' roses, larkspur, pink spray carnations, tulips and alstroemeria.

A modern arrangement
A dramatic modern arrangement of quality flowers offers something very different for Mother's Day. The glass vase shows off the Arum italicum, *gerberas and double tulips to perfection.*

Child's posy

A delightful design for a child to give is this dainty but colourful selection of anemones, muscari and foliage, tied up with a large ribbon bow.

Hostess bouquet

Any mother would be thrilled to receive this wonderful selection of 'Jacaranda' roses, gerberas, nerines, alstroemeria, gypsophila and bear grass, tied into an all-round hostess bouquet.

Planted basket

A traditional rustic basket has been lined with polythene and moss and then planted with three primrose plants. The daffodils and muscari were put in a small container of water.

VALENTINE'S DAY

Valentine's Day can be fun, as it is a light-hearted celebration, and the one day in the year when customers are predominantly male. It is important to make them feel comfortable, for although there are many 'new men', there are still those who find it embarrassing to buy and to carry flowers. For many male customers, this may be the first time they have been in a florist's shop.

It is often hard to explain to customers why the price of red roses can rise so dramatically on this day, but nurseries can only grow a certain number of roses, and are not able to stockpile them, due to their perishable nature. When you then consider the massive demand for red roses, it is much easier to understand why they command a premium price at auctions and markets.

Everyone wants flowers for his sweetheart to be delivered on the day itself or the previous evening, so prior preparation is crucial if you want a successful Valentine's Day. Always keep records of peak periods; these can be a valuable reference when ordering and preparing for the following year. Start early with preparations, as this will help to ensure a smooth-running and stress-free Valentine's Day.

Modern style
This modern design of fresh bright greens combines three red roses with gerberas, carnation sprays, hellebores, and a selection of foliage types, including a lovely hosta.

From the heart
A heart-shaped vase is complemented by this tiny posy of anemones and red carnation sprays. The striped gift paper has been taken around and into the centre of the design.

Classical bouquet

Gypsophila and asparagus fern give this classic handtied bouquet, with its red roses and carnation sprays, a soft and dainty finish and an old-fashioned feel.

Only a rose

A single red rose, dressed up with pretty heart-patterned ribbon, is a beautiful way to say 'I love you'.

Stargazer

This very special cellophane-wrapped bouquet of mixed flowers contains three red roses and some 'Stargazer' lilies, which have a wonderful fragrance. Hearts on the cellophane provide a romantic finishing touch.

A VALENTINE'S WINDOW

Window displays should aim to catch the customers' attention and drag them into the shop. Something in the display will capture the imagination and encourage an impulse buy. Certain occasions, such as Christmas or Valentine's Day, are very traditional in flavour, and we tend to turn out the same designs year after year, without perhaps giving enough thought to the matter.

Next Valentine's Day, why not try something a little different, creating an alternative Valentine's Day display to appeal to the younger generation?

Colour

Traditional Valentine's arrangements are red, but why not ring the changes and add some purple and violet shades? This gives the designs a dramatic visual impact, which should appeal to many people.

Style

The arrangements pictured here have been made in a European style, and while their modern look is angled at the younger generation, encouraging them to start the flower-buying habit for Valentine's Day, these designs could be equally appealing for other occasions, such as Mother's Day or Christmas. Their stark simplicity makes them eye-catching and therefore ideal for a window display. Keep designs simple and colourful, and you will have a winning display on your hands.

An alternative Valentine's window display – tall upright, handtied, parallel and split-level styles of design, together with a basket, combine to create an unusual and eye-catching promotion. The display is aimed at the younger generation, for whom the bold colours and striking designs have much appeal.

Display accessories

These must be incorporated into the complete window display, not added as an afterthought. They must, in effect, form part of the overall balance, and while they are useful, they should not overshadow a display.

It is helpful to keep a stock of accessories that can be changed from time to time to keep the display interesting. Never overdo the amount of accessories, or the window may look jumbled. Be adventurous and daring, and you will stop your customers in their tracks.

Shapes and textures

In modern arrangements, the shape of the individual flowers is very important – they must be bold and dramatic. Texture is also important when so few flowers are used, but the most essential feature is space.

Valentine's Day accessories

Wholesalers offer florists a wide range of accessories to add a personal touch to Valentine designs. Cellophane wrap is used throughout the year, but for Valentine's Day you can make an arrangement even more special by using cellophane wrap with hearts and motifs on.

There is also a wide selection of picks and motifs, ranging from plastic cupids and hearts to dainty pottery, glass figures and delicate lace accessories. This includes plastic and pottery containers at prices to suit all pockets.

It is vital to be well-prepared for any peak selling period. Arrangements of fabric flowers can be organized well in advance and stored ready for the great day. A window display will require no maintenance if made with fabric flowers

CHRISTMAS

The florist is *the* Christmas specialist. The shop is a treasure trove of gifts, displaying for the customer an endless selection of Christmas tree decorations, novelties, toys, lovely ribbons, specialized artificial Christmas flowers and foliage, plus a range of beautiful flowering and foliage house plants. In addition, of course, the florist offers an extensive service of ready-made designs for purchase as gifts or to decorate homes, shops, offices and hotels.

The florist is helped to capture the magic of Christmas by a range of wholesalers who now offer delightful Christmas stock, including white and natural teddies, complete with Christmas scarves and hats, ready to be gift-wrapped for children or adults, or incorporated into arrangements. Special Christmas lines such as Victorian boxes sell well. Baskets are always popular, and can be sold as individual presents or filled with artificial or fresh materials, to make a complete gift.

Preparations
Carefully thought-out and well-organized preparation is essential if you are to meet the needs of this busy selling time.

- Clearing stock rooms creates storage space for the Christmas stock.
- Tidy workrooms, offices, chillers and cellars to gain maximum working and storage space.
- Plan shop window and interior displays so that special props and display stands are made in advance.
- Clean and re-organize the shop to give extra display and serving areas.
- To gain maximum interest, Christmas merchandise can be put on display in late October/early November.
- All stock must be clearly priced; staff must know every product, where it is displayed, and its name, use and price.
- The shop must always look attractive and full. Display areas and shelves must constantly be tidied and restocked to tempt customers to buy.
- During November, Christmas designs made with dried and fabric materials can be prepared, as can bows for gift wrapping.
- Nearer Christmas, prepare planted bowls and decorate holly wreaths, crosses and door garlands.

- Serving areas must be stocked with wrapping/packing equipment and order pads.
- During the hectic Christmas rush, courteous, friendly and knowledgeable salestaff in the florist's shop can make Christmas shopping a pleasure.

Christmas tree decorations
Traditionally decorated with multicoloured lights and ornaments, the tree is now frequently colour-coordinated, to blend with the room decor of a private home or a business. A further development is the 'theme tree', decorated with ornaments and garlands representing themes such as a toy shop, Victorian times or a winter frost.

The florist will not only offer a tree decorating service, but will arrange a complete floral decoration scheme for hotels, shops, business premises or private homes. Door garlands are covered later in this section; swags may decorate stairs or mantelpieces, with fresh and artificial foliage being given the designer touch by the addition of beautiful ribbons and Christmas novelties.

Picks and sprays
Each Christmas season witnesses a new theme added to the 'pick'. Picks of foliage now include presents, birds and nests, fruit, nuts or musical instruments. Artificial sprays of flowers, foliage, nuts and fruits look so natural that the customer often has difficulty in choosing.

Fresh flowers and pot plants
A wide range of beautiful and dramatic pot plants, such as poinsettias and flowers, that have been specially prepared to flower ahead of their natural season, is available at this time of year. These make lovely gifts for the Christmas hostess or decorations for the festive home.

The florist is the best supplier of quality flowers and foliage plants that have been well conditioned and prepared for sale. The Christmas stock now includes a fascinating range of plants, flowers and foliage from all over the world.

Christmas is not just a time for red and green – this arrangement was made on a foam base and uses bold groupings of materials for a refreshing change.

WINTER WEDDINGS

Velvet, muffs, bare trees and churches set in wintry landscapes – this is the imagery of a winter wedding. Winter brides tend to choose dresses in warm velvets, heavy brocades or light-weight wools, with rich colours for the bridesmaids, including scarlet and crimson, sapphire blue, bottle green, and tartans.

Flowers favoured by winter brides include amaryllis (Hippeastrum hybrids), *Anemone coronaria*, azaleas, Christmas roses *(Helleborus niger)*, *Euphorbia fulgens*, freesia hybrids, poinsettias *(Euphorbia pulcherrima)* and *Ranunculus asiaticus.*

Styles of design

The range of designs to bear in mind for a winter wedding include the following: for the bride – muff sprays, traditional and European-style bouquets and posies, over-arm bouquets and hostess bouquets; for an adult bridesmaid – muff sprays, prayer book sprays, traditional and European-style bouquets and posies, hostess bouquets and baskets, and for young bridesmaids – open/ Victorian posies, natural posies, baskets, hoops and pomanders. Headdresses may be garlands, or side or back placements.

WHAT YOU WILL NEED

A selection of good quality well-conditioned flowers and foliage, selection of stub and reel wires, tapes, satin ribbon (for handles), gold cord, millinery wire for headdress, bouquet stand, and floristry tools.

The basic straight shower bouquet for the bride contains 'Mont Blanc' lilies, 'Coronet' roses, 'Grace' freesias and 'Butterscotch' alstroemerias. The foliage types used were jasmine and ivy trails, bear grass, dogwood (Cornus) stems, Leycesteria and Garrya elliptica. Loops of gold cord link with embroidery on the bride's dress.

The bridesmaid is carrying an open posy and wearing a garland headdress. Both contain roses, freesias, alstroemerias and hydrangeas, together with a selection of foliage types similar to those of the bride's bouquet. Focus the colours, flowers and design on the dresses of the bride and bridesmaids to create a harmonious visual impression.

Coordinating colours, flowers and designs should be suggested to the bride. Here, the bride will have a matching cape with hood trimmed with fur, and the bridesmaid will wear a burgundy velvet cloak.

SYMPATHY AND MEMORIAL

Memorial designs are often taken to the graveside at Christmas to express love and respect, and to offer comfort to the bereaved. The use of evergreens for Christmas decorations is a traditional practice that dates back to ancient times, and from the florist's viewpoint, holly wreaths and crosses offer a practical alternative to cut flowers placed in cemetary vases, with the advantage that, at a time of year when the elements can quickly damage flowers, evergreens will withstand wind and cold – even frost and snow – and remain attractive for a long time. Cones and clusters of bright red berries are lasting alternatives to the carnations used here.

WHAT YOU WILL NEED

Variegated holly, gold cupressus, *Skimmia japonica*, larch cones, red carnations, sphagnum moss, stub wires, foam bump, and a foam cross frame.

Mechanics and method

Wreaths and crosses made with evergreens are normally assembled using traditional mossed frames, which can withstand considerable handling, but now that foam bases are increasingly available, the latter are also becoming common for these seasonal designs.

A point to remember when using foam bases is to insert the holly firmly. Added security is given if the sprigs of holly at vulnerable points are mounted with stub wires before insertion.

Foliages

In this design, cupressus has been used to form the outline. If gold cupressus is not available, a surprisingly good effect is achieved by lightly spraying green cupressus with a yellow spray paint. The lovely foliage and larch cones used in the cluster will still look attractive long after the carnations have succumbed to the elements.

1 *The foam has first been lightly soaked with water. A foam bump, similarly prepared, is attached for the cluster, and a foliage outline of gold cupressus has been inserted.*

2 *A creamy variegated holly has been added to the gold cupressus and, to increase the textured look, sphagnum moss and* Skimmia japonica *flowers have been inserted.*

3 *Rich red carnations, larch cones and foliage make a striking cluster. The outer materials are placed in the foam, followed by the focal flowers at the centre.*

The final placement of red carnations and foliage completes the cross, which displays a striking contrast between the vivid red carnations and creamy holly.

DOOR GARLANDS

After the tree, the door garland or wreath is the most popular festive design. Its cheerful colours and pungent aroma of pine offer a true seasonal welcome.

Many people prefer to keep to traditional materials, such as holly, mistletoe and ivy, and to colours such as red and green, but to show that it is possible to incorporate other materials and colours, the garland in the main picture suggests an alternative Christmas theme. The moss frame has been covered in golden cupressus, and golden apples and mandarins were wired in groups and firmly attached to the frame. They are interspersed with pine cones, bread knots and tartan ribbons. The result is a bright and cheerful wreath to greet visitors.

Door garlands are a traditional symbol of welcome and hospitality, dating back to ancient Persia. The Greeks also used garlands or wreaths made from greenery such as olive or laurel in their ancient Olympic games, and laurel is still used in the victors' chaplets. In those times, evergreen plant materials were an obvious choice for

1 *The wire frame is mossed and backed with wreath wrap, and fans of cupressus are then added as an edging. The cupressus fans are made with 0.90mm (20 gauge) wires, 18cm (6 ¾in) long, pushed firmly into the moss.*

WHAT YOU WILL NEED

Cupressus and trims of your choice, 0.56mm binding wire, 0.90mm (20 gauge) stub wires, moss, and wreath wrap.

---

wreaths, as many cultures worshipped evergreens such as laurel, mistletoe or holly.

To present-day florists, the advantage of garlands is that they keep fresh throughout the festive season. Whatever the end use of a garland, be adventurous in your ideas and try out unusual combinations, making designs that are unique, bold and stunning.

Bases

A traditional base of moss wired onto a frame is still the most popular way of forming a garland, but materials such as straw, vines, wisteria and honeysuckle make wonderful alternatives, and have the additional bonus of needing no wire frame.

Whatever the frame, it can be decorated with a wide variety of materials, including nuts, cones, berries, apples, tangerines, kumquats, and even fungi.

2 *The moss is covered with small pieces of cupressus, hairpinned into place. A range of sample trims is shown. These include holly, pine cones and red velvet ribbon, tartan ribbon and cones, ribbon and red apples, sprayed larch cones and a robin.*

A bright and cheerful design offers a warm welcome to Christmas guests.

CHRISTMAS DISPLAY

Christmas is a magical time, and as florists we must capture that magic in our displays. Garlands, swags and door wreaths are still top of the Christmas shopping list. Why not update garlands with tartan bows, and swags with paper ribbons? Add fruit, nuts and gourds to door wreaths. Use exciting golds, greens, silver and blues as well as the traditional red.

Shop displays are often disappointing, reflecting an unplanned presentation of goods. Time is given to more demanding areas of work, resulting in what should be an advertisement, working 24 hours a day for the business, doing exactly the opposite. Display is an art form in three dimensions, with ideas used to attract customers to enter and buy. Window display has to be composed like a picture and, as in a picture, it is advisable to confine the objects displayed within a narrower space than the window frame itself. Novelty always stops people in their tracks, so why not use an accessory, such as the fireplace shown opposite, to attract attention?

The majority of goods need to be at eye level or below, as it is easier to look down than up. Good lighting is also important but it has to be discreet as the public should see the well-lit display not the lights.

Candles

The candles in the picture have been lit for the photograph only – it is dangerous to use naked flames, especially near artificial materials, and customers should be advised that candles are for display only. Always attach a 'Do not light candles' label to any display containing them.

Display guidelines

Forward planning is important; a good display should be planned with these questions in mind:

Why – Christmas, Valentine's Day, Mother's Day
Where – shop windows, island stands
What – fresh flowers, containers or sundries

Balance is an important factor. There should be a visual framework to attract the eye and make the display look pleasing. Presentation is equally important. Price tickets and display cards should be written neatly and clearly. Window display can become time-consuming, so keep it simple. The colour theme and accessories can be chosen well in advance, and fresh plants and flowers added at the last minute.

The essential ingredient is imagination – make your display vibrant, colourful and exciting, and it will sell your flowers. People automatically respond to colour, especially in the world of flowers, so use colour themes to give impact to your displays and to stimulate ideas and interest.

Above *The shiny red basket gives the planted arrangement a truly Christmassy feel.*
Right *A large mahogany fireplace provides the background to these classic Christmas designs, the rich green and gold garland framing the wreath mantelpiece arrangement and the swag.*

AROUND THE WORLD

We see so many exciting and different flowers from around the world in our shops, it is intriguing to see the diverse kinds of designs that florists in other countries construct.

Around the world, flowers are used in very much the same way and for the same reasons – for celebrations, as gifts, to say thank-you, for pleasure, as a decoration, and in times of sorrow. In every country, there are national superstitions and traditions linked with individual flowers, and wherever a florist might be, he or she will soon acquire this information, and will know the correct designs and flower materials to suggest to customers for particular occasions. Failure to do so may cause offence

Design variations

Most of the flowers seen in florist's shops are available across the world. These 'international' flowers include the rose, the carnation, the lily and the chrysanthemum spray, and there are many others. The seasonal flowers and foliage of each country will vary, however, and it is these, along with design variations, that make national arrangements so interesting.

Each country and even regions within some countries have different ways of designing with flowers. In the designs here, we can only give a 'flavour' of the continents, and the way in which flowers are designed in each, together with the types of flowers and colours used.

New Zealand and Australia

Kangaroo paw and New Zealand flax are perhaps the florist's most obvious choices of plant material, but to interpret the sub-tropics, with its lush greens was a refreshing alternative.

Asia

This simple yet lovely design is a perfect example of the style of arranging flowers in Asia. Peonies have been in cultivation in China for over a thousand years, but did not arrive in Europe until 1808.

America
Colour is the important element of
this arrangement, in which
the red, white and blue of
the American flag are
teamed with balloons and
'ticker tape' streamers.

Europe
Larkspurs, roses and
Dutch iris are used in
this arrangement, which
combines flavours from several
European countries.

Africa
This handtied design suits a land
of strong contrasts, evoking the
exotic and lush jungles
with the hot plains
and tall elephant
grass.

CUT FLOWER CARE

Names	Stage to buy	Vase life	Conditioning methods	Remarks
Acacia spp Mimosa	1/2 florets open	About 4 – 5 days	Warm water treatment; flower food for shrubs; remove wrap *after* full conditioning	Spicy scent; mimosa can be dried
Aconitum Monkshood	1/3 florets open	8 – 10 days	Warm water treatment; cut flower food	No scent; poisonous; ethylene sensitive
Agapanthus africanus African lily, Lily of the Nile	1/4 florets open	10 – 15 days	Warm water treatment; cut flower food	No scent; too cold or over-long cold storage will lead to bud drop
Alchemilla mollis Lady's mantle	Most flowers open	10 – 12 days	Tepid water treatment; cut flower food for herbaceous flowers	No scent
Allium spp Onion	Almost fully mature	10 – 20 days, depending on cultivar	Tepid water treatment; cut flower food for bulb flowers	A slight onion scent; can be dried
Alstroemeria spp Peruvian lily	4/5 florets open	10 – 12 days	Warm water treatment; cut flower food for herbaceous flowers	No scent; ethylene sensitive; foliage is very brittle
Amaranthus caudatus Love-lies-bleeding	Almost fully developed	6 – 10 days	Warm water treatment; cut flower food for herbaceous flowers	No scent; can be dried
Ammi majus Lace flower	1/3 florets open	6 – 8 days	Warm water treatment; cut flower food for herbaceous flowers	No scent
Anemone coronaria Windflower	Buds starting to open	5 – 8 days	Remove white part of stem; warm water treatment; cut flower food for bulb flowers	No scent
Anthurium andreanum Tail flower; painter's palette	Spadix almost fully mature	10 – 15 days; red flowers have the shortest life	Remove vial of water, cut stem; warm water treatment; immerse wilted flowers for 1 – 2 hours; no cut flower food required	No scent; storage above 13°C (56°F) or physical damage will result in the spathe turning blue
Antirrhinum majus Snapdragon	3 florets fully open	8 – 10 days	Tepid water treatment; cut flower food	No scent; ethylene sensitive; stems will bend upwards when used horizontally
Asparagus setaceus (*A. plumosus*) Asparagus fern	Mature stems	10 – 14 days	Remove white part of stem; tepid water; no cut flower food required	No scent
Aster novi-belgi Michaelmas daisy; Aster	Most flowers open	8 – 10 days	Warm water treatment; cut flower food	Slight scent
Aster ericoides 'Monte Casino'	Most flowers open	8 – 10 days	Warm water treatment; cut flower food	No scent
Astilbe spirea Astilbe hybrids	Most flowers open	4 – 6 days	Warm water treatment; cut flower food	No scent

Names	Stage to buy	Vase life	Conditioning methods	Remarks
Bouvardia spp Bouvardia	1/2 florets open	10 – 15 days	Warm water treatment; use special bouvardia cut flower food; avoid a dry atmosphere	Slight scent; will suffer easily from dehydration; priority conditioning; advise customers to put in water quickly
Campanula spp Canterbury bells; bellflower	1/2 florets open	8 – 12 days	Warm water treatment; cut flower food for herbaceous flowers	No scent
Cattleya spp Orchid	Fully open	7 – 10 days; pollination shortens vase life	Warm water treatment; cut flower food	Slight scent; ethylene sensitive; cold sensitive below 13°C (56°F)
Chrysanthemum hybrids Florists' chrysanthemum	Spray – 3/4 florets open; blooms; outer petals fully out	14 – 21days; outdoor, 7 – 10 days	Remove woody portion of stem; tepid water treatment – warm for outdoor flowers; cut flower food	Aromatic
Chrysanthemum parthenium Feverfew	1/2 florets open	10 – 15 days	Tepid water treatment; cut flower food for herbaceous flowers	Scent is similar to camomile
Convallaria majalis Lily of the valley	1/2 florets open	4 – 5 days; slightly longer outdoors	Remove roots from indoor grown flowers; tepid water treatment; cut flower food	A wonderful perfume; keep cool
Curcuma roscoeana Hidden lily	Bracts showing good colour	15 – 20 days	Warm water treatment; cut flower food	Slight scent
Cymbidium spp Orchid	On stem; when most flowers are open	2 – 4 weeks; pollination shortens vase life	Warm water treatment; cut flower food	No scent; cold sensitive below 8°C (46°F)
Cytisus x *praecox* Broom	Buds showing good colour	5 – 8 days	Warm water treatment; cut flower food for shrubs	Unpleasant scent
Dahlia spp Dahlia	Fully open	6 – 10 days, depending on cultivar	Warm water treatment; cut flower food	Aromatic; foliage will pollute the water
Delphinium consolida Larkspur	Several florets open	8 – 10 days	Tepid water treatment; cut flower food	No scent; ethylene sensitive; can be dried
Delphinium hybrids Delphinium	1/2 florets open	8 – 10 days	Warm water treatment; cut flower food	No scent; ethylene sensitive
Dianthus barbatus Sweet William	1/2 florets open	7 – 10 days	Warm water treatment; cut flower food for herbaceous flowers	Slight scent
Dianthus caryophyllus Carnation	Standards half or almost fully open; 2/3 fully open for sprays	5 – 10 days; longer in cool temperature	Cut between the nodes; warm water treatment; cut flower food	Some have a lovely fragrance; ethylene sensitive
Eremus hybrids Foxtail lily	1/3 or 1/2 florets open	10 – 15 days	Warm water treatment; cut flower food	No scent
Euphorbia fulgens Spurge; scarlet plume	Showing plenty of colour	8 – 10 days	Hot water treatment to seal latex; cut flower food at ½ strength to prevent foliage from yellowing	No scent; ethylene and cold sensitive; do not store below 10°C (50°F); will suffer from dehydration
Eustoma grandiflora Lisianthus	3 – 4 open florets	Individual flowers will last five days; buds will develop over 1 – 2 weeks	Tepid water treatment; cut flower food for herbaceous flowers	No scent; stems need regular recutting

Names	Stage to buy	Vase life	Conditioning methods	Remarks
Forsythia spp Golden bell	Buds showing colour, unless for forcing	10 – 15 days	Warm water treatment; cut flower food for shrubs	Slight fragrance
Freesia hybrids Freesia	First floret in bud, but showing good colour	7 – 10 days, longer if spent florets removed	Warm water treatment	Very sweetly scented; ethylene sensitive
Gerbera jamesonii Transvaal or Barberton lily	Outer stamens showing pollen; look for firm stems	5 – 19 days, depending on bacteria in the water	Needs to be kept upright while conditioning; warm water treatment; cut flower food	No scent; very sensitive to bacteria in the water; susceptible to grey mould
Gladiolus spp Sword lily; bridal gladioli	One floret open and 3 – 4 buds showing colour	12 – 20 days, depending on the cultivar; remove spent florets	Tepid water treatment; cut flower food for bulb flowers	No scent; ethylene sensitive
Gypsophila paniculata Gyp; baby's breath	Florets open but not overly mature	Up to 14 days	Cut between the nodes; warm water treatment; cut flower food for herbaceous flowers	No scent; can be dried
Helianthus annus Sunflower	Fully open flowers	5 – 10 days	Warm water treatment; cut flower food	No scent; can be dried
Heliconia spp Lobster claw	Flower buds well coloured	8 – 28 days, depending on the cultivar	Warm water treatment; cut flower food	No scent; cold sensitive below 10°C (50°F)
Hippeastrum hybrids Amaryllis lily	Well coloured buds	10 – 14 days	Warm water treatment; cut flower food for bulb flowers	No scent; cold sensitive below 12°C (54°F)
Iris hollandica Dutch iris	Buds well coloured, with petals emerging	3 – 8 days, depending on the temperature	Tepid water treatment; cut flower food for bulb flowers	No scent – late season iris have second buds that will develop
Kniphofia spp Red hot poker; torch lily	Most florets showing colour	8 – 10 days	Tepid water treatment; cut flower food	No scent; ethylene sensitive; stems will bend upwards when used horizontally
Liatris spp Gayfeather	1/2 florets open	10 – 12 days	Warm water treatment; cut flower food	No scent; can be dried
Lilium spp Lily	1/2 buds showing good colour	8 – 14 days	Warm water treatment; cut flower food at ½ strength	Lovely heavy fragrance from most cultivars; remove the stamens, as the pollen can stain
Matthiola incana Stock	6/10 florets open	5 – 10 days; change water frequently	Tepid water treatment; cut flower food	Strong scent; ethylene sensitive
Narcissus spp Daffodil	At the goose neck stage	6 – 10 days, but less at high temperatures	Tepid water treatment; cut flower food for bulb flowers; do not mix with other flowers until they have been conditioned for 24 hours	Most cultivars have a fragrance; ethylene sensitive; stems exude a sap that can be harmful to other flowers
Nerine bowdenii Nerine	Oldest buds almost open	12 – 15 days	Warm water treatment; cut flower food for bulbs	No scent; cold sensitive below 12°C (54°F)
Paeonia Peony	Buds showing colour	10 – 15 days	Warm water treatment; cut flower food	Some cultivars are very fragrant

Names	Stage to buy	Vase life	Conditioning methods	Remarks
Papaver spp Poppy	Buds just showing colour	3 – 7 days	Hot water treatment to seal stems; cut flower food for herbaceous flowers	No scent; seed heads can be dried
Phalaenopsis spp Moth orchid	Most flowers on stem open	14 – 20 days	Tepid water treatment; cut flower food	No scent; ethylene sensitive
Proteaceae Protia, Banksia and others	Mature flowers	10 – 25 days depending on species	Hot water treatment; cut flower food for shrub flowers	No scent; some proteaceae are cold sensitive below 8°C (45°F); can be dried
Rosa hybrids Rose	Important in winter and autumn for buds to show good colour	8 – 10 days, depending on cultivar	Tepid water (warm water in winter); cut flower food	Some cultivars have a lovely scent; ethylene and bacteria sensitive
Solidago spp Golden rod	1/2 florets open	7 – 10 days	Tepid water; cut flower food	No scent; can be dried
Stephanotis floribunda Madagascar jasmine	Mature flowers; avoid any with 'spotting'	2 – 4 days	Remove from plastic bag; put into shallow water with cut flower food	Very fragrant
Strelitzia reginae Bird of paradise	First floret open	12 – 15 days; remove spent florets	Warm water treatment; cut flower food	No scent; may need help to open flowers; gently lift outer petals from the pod
Syringa spp Lilac	First florets open	8 – 12 days	Warm water treatment; cut flower food for shrub flowers	A lovely fragrance
Trachelium spp Throatwort	Flowers almost fully open	8 – 10 days	Tepid water treatment; cut flower food	No scent; ethylene sensitive
Triteleia laxa Brodiaea	4 florets open	10 – 12 days	Tepid water treatment; cut flower food for bulb flowers	No scent
Tulipa spp Tulip	Darwin hybrids – when bud is half coloured; other cultivars – when buds are fully coloured	5 – 7 days	Tepid water treatment; cut flower food for bulb flowers; store vertically to prevent bending	No scent; stems will bend upward when used horizontally; stems continue to grow and elongate after cutting
Urceolina amazonica (*Eucharis grandiflora*) Amazon lily	One floret open	6 – 8 days	Tepid water treatment; cut flower food for bulb flowers	A delicate scent; cold sensitive below 12°C (54°F)
Viburnum opulus 'Sterile' Snowball tree	Still green	10 – 12 days	Warm water treatment; cut flower food for shrubs	No scent
Zantedeschia spp Calla, Arum lily	As the spathe begins to turn downward	8 – 10 days; longer in cool temperatures	Tepid water treatment; cut flower food	Slight scent; an elastic band will prevent the stem end from splitting in the vase
Zingiberaceae Ginger	Bracts showing good colour	2 – 3 weeks, depending on cultivar	Warm water treatment; cut flower food	Slight spicy scent; soak wilted stems in warm water for a short amount of time; cold sensitive

GLOSSARY

All round arrangement An arrangement that is viewed from all sides; suitable for a table centre.

Anniversary arrangement An arrangement for a wedding anniversary celebration, often taking its colour from the name of the anniversary; for example ruby, silver, or gold.

Asymmetrical arrangement An L-shaped design with one side wider than the other. The design is balanced by the use of heavier materials on the short side, and finer materials on the long side.

Backing A method of covering the back of a moss tribute to keep in the moisture and make it more pleasant to handle; the upper surface is left free to receive stems.

Bacteria A living organism that builds up in vase water and blocks the flower stems, restricting the water uptake in flowers.

Balance The use of flowers or foliage and colour to achieve both an actual and visual effect of stability.

Beidermeyer A small tied bunch of flowers; the stems are spiralled and the top of the design is flat.

Boutonnière A small group of flowers and foliage mounted together, this design is worn by both men and women.

Bouquet A formal design, either for carrying at a wedding ceremony or for presentation and subsequent carrying in public.

Branching unit The unit of one type of material is assembled in a branching manner, with short, taped 'stems'; graduation in size is important.

Buttonhole A single flower – a carnation, for example – backed by foliage.

Container A receptacle, containing foam or water, into which flowers are arranged.

Conditioning The treatment of flowers upon arrival from the market, to encourage water uptake.

Corsage A selection of prepared materials, assembled into a design suitable for personal adornment.

Cut flower food A substance added to water to extend the vase life of cut flowers.

Ethylene gas A colourless gas, it is given off by fruit and vegetables and causes flowers to mature quickly.

External wiring A wire is inserted into the base of the flower head and is wound around the stem.

Exotics Flowers, foliage types or seed pods imported from abroad and unusual in texture or shape are termed exotics; these include protea, banksia, ginger and kangaroo paw.

Focal point The central point of a design, from which all stems appear to radiate.

Garland Fresh or dried flowers and foliage, bound onto a rope or wire frame; traditionally used to decorate mantelpieces, marquee poles and top tables.

Greening Giving a covering of foliage to plastic foam, ready for a flower arrangement.

Internal wiring The support wire is inserted into the stem so that it is concealed.

Mounting The addition of a wire to the stem end, to give anchorage.

Mossing Binding moss onto a frame, using binding wire.

Natural unit Two or three flowers or foliage stems, mounted together.

Plant material This includes flowers, foliage, grasses, and seed heads, both dried and fresh.

Plastic foam Preformed shapes of foam that are used as a foundation for flowers.

Semi-internal wiring A wire inserted into the stem, 5cm (2in) below the head and wound around the stem.

Sheaf A bunch of flowers, tied together with the stems spiralling; normally used as a funeral tribute.

Stub wire This is used to support flowers and foliage, especially in wedding work; stub wires come in a variety of gauges and lengths.

Support wiring The addition of a wire to strengthen the stem.

Topiary tree A tree that has been formally clipped into an ornamental shape; the shape is used when making fresh and dried arrangements to decorate tables or marquees, for example.

Wreath A circular shape in foam or moss, used as a funeral tribute.

Wiring The use of wire for support, control and anchorage of plant material.

INDEX

ACKNOWLEDGEMENTS

This achievement is not ours alone. It owes much to the help and encouragement we have received from many people. We are grateful to our families, friends, colleagues and to those who are mentioned below:

Mr Gordon Limb, Principal, for the use of the extensive facilities and gardens at the Welsh College of Horticulture;
Wendy Robinson, who was really the fourth member of our team and an inspriation to us all;
Lesley Booth, Jo Green, who designed with a smile, and our students of 1992/3, who willingly provided both their time and their talents;
Karl Adamson, our marvellous photographer, Diana Lodge, our patient and supportive editor, Paul Cooper, our designer, and Heather Dewhurst, managing editor at Merehurst, many thanks for your encouragement and help and finally, the staff at the Celyn Plant Centre, Marion Hunt and the catering staff who looked after us so well.

For this revised edition we welcomed the help and many talents of Stephen Roberts, Jo Green, Paul Raven and, again, our special photographer, Karl Adamson. Many thanks to our enthusiastic and cheerful commissioning editor, Karen Hemingway. Finally, we wish to acknowledge the support of Dr Mark Simkin, current Principal, who allowed us once again to use the facilities at the Welsh College.

We would also like to thank the following people and companies for supplying their products:

Naylor Bases Ltd
Val Spicer Designs
Smithers Oasis UK Ltd
Chrysal Ltd
Vitabrick
Bouquet Products Ltd

Douthwaite Florists Sundries Ltd
Bloomfix Wetfoam Products
Triflora Floral Foams
Roger Lyon, Periwinkle Supplies Ltd, Deeside
Sue Taylor, The Flower Boutique, Wallasey
Martin Lewis, N.J. Cook & Sons, St Asaph